THE PONY BREEDER'S COMPANION

THE PONY BREEDER'S COMPANION

A Guide for Owners and Breeders

Caroline Nesbitt

HOWELL
BOOK
HOUSE

NEW YORK

Photographs by Caroline Nesbitt unless otherwise credited.

Howell Book House
A Simon & Schuster Macmillan Company
1633 Broadway
New York, NY 10019

MACMILLAN is a registered trademark of Macmillan, Inc.

Library of Congress Cataloging-in-Publication Data

Nesbitt, Caroline,
        The pony breeder's companion: a guide for owners and breeders/Caroline Nesbitt.
            p.   cm.
        Includes bibliographical references and index.
        ISBN 0-87605-996-5
        1. Ponies—Breeding. 2. Ponies. I. Title.
SF315.N47 1995
636.1'6—dc20   95-15647
                                              CIP

Manufactured in the United States of America

10 9 8 7 6 5 4 3 2 1

CONTENTS

Acknowledgments

No project of this size would be possible without the generous help of numerous people. My thanks are due to the following breeders, judges, professionals, veterinarians, and pony owners who patiently responded to my questions, willingly delved into studbooks, supplied me with history, photos, and materials, and shared ideas and opinions with me over the course of the last few months:

Sherrie Ackerman Ballou, Charles Ballou, Fern Bittner, A. Sandra Davis, Mrs. A. R. Dunning, Ann S. Fisher, Eve Fout, Jeri Freels, Lendon F. Gray, Jacqueline Harris, Stephen O. Hawkins, Joel and Meg Hempel, Patty Hyyppa, Maureen Lapicola, Catherine Mack, Matthew MacKay-Smith, DVM, Boo McDaniel, Randy McCoy, Marian E. Molthan, Jim Roberts, farrier Bill Sugg, Cherry Wilson, Kristine A. Woodaman, DVM, and all of the friends and pony lovers who have been enthusiastic and encouraging about the need for this book.

Also I would like to thank the friendly people whose brains I picked at the American Horse Shows Association, American Driving Society, American Livestock Breeds Conservancy, U.S. Combined Training Association, U.S. Dressage Federation, and all the breed societies whose ponies have been profiled here. If I've left anyone out, please forgive me and believe that it was not in any way intentional!

Additional thanks are owed to Robin Bledsoe, Bookseller; Linda Haines, her husband, Scott McGuffin, and their son,

Dylan; India Haynes of Waterford Welsh Cobs in Maine; Anne Holmes of Marlyn Exmoors in Nova Scotia; Hope Garland Ingersoll, Bunny Ramsay, and Lisa Leland-Courschenes of Grazing Fields Farm, Ltd., in Massachusetts; Layne and Ed Keller; Pat Kimura of Someday Farm (and ADS) in Michigan; Fran O'Reilly; Pat Fisher Pawlowicz of Grand Prix Farm in Massachusetts; photographer Stan Phaneuf; Carol Rivoire of Beaver Dam Fjords in Nova Scotia; Connie Tuor of Windfall Stables in Oregon; Mr. and Mrs. Lyle Thompson of Thompson's Haflinger Farm in New Hampshire; and Wilhelmine Waller of Tanrackin Farm in New York. They all cheerfully went the extra mile for me when I asked and reinforced my feeling that pony people are as generous as the ponies they raise.

Finally, this book is for R., because he believed, and Alex, because he drove me back to my typewriter.

INTRODUCTION

Ponies in the United States have become big business. Registries for major breeds such as the Connemara, Welsh, Shetland, Norwegian Fjord, Haflinger, and Pony of the Americas have a combined membership of more than thirteen thousand, with the number of ponies registered (and frequently owned by nonmembers of the governing societies) often approaching three or four times that number. The American Horse Shows Association (AHSA) has records for nearly fifteen hundred ponies that won at least one point in their annual Horse of the Year awards standings in the Pony Hunter divisions alone in 1994. These figures don't include the additional number that compete variously in the pony section of the Children's Hunter division, Pony Medal (equitation), Welsh, Hackney, or Shetland divisions. They can't even begin to reflect the number of ponies that compete on the Zone, Regional, Local, or 4-H levels in Leadline, Short Stirrup, Walk-Trot, Maiden and Novice Equitation, or the vast number that compete regularly in Pony Club, combined training, or driving. And of course it cannot encompass the number of ponies that are used lovingly year after year in school programs and in backyards as companions and teachers for young children at levels of experience ranging from the first slow walk with a parent to the upper levels of competition.

Ponies are also rapidly gaining popularity as the mount of choice for any number of dedicated adult amateurs, whether they are recreational trail riders, avid hunters, or regular competitors in disciplines that do not restrict equine entrants by height. The opening up of All Breeds competition in dressage and combined training, coupled with a surge in popularity of Adult Amateur divisions at horse shows, has given ponies a further boost as suitable competitive mounts for adults as well as children. The U.S. Combined Training Association estimates that as many as 20 percent of its membership consists of juniors and adults who ride ponies or pony crosses. And the American Driving Society estimates that upwards of 30 percent of its membership competes with ponies, with pony divisions at their sanctioned meets frequently better filled than those restricted to horses. Numerous established breeders further maintain that in recent years the calls they receive most often come from people who say something such as, "I'm forty-five and five-foot-two, and I want something a lot smaller than my last horse. Something sensible that I can have fun on and that won't eat me out of house and home." This equals potential good times for the serious pony breeder.

Yet all too often, ponies are treated like second-class citizens in the greater world of sport horse breeding, even in the face of their continued popularity, variety of uses, and undeniable talents. This was illustrated to me all too clearly a few years ago when I was looking for a nice little Thoroughbred mare to breed to our pony stallion so that we could try our hand with a few halfbreds. Nearly everywhere I looked, and nearly everybody I talked to, had the same response: "Well, you won't care what she is, *because you only want to breed her to your pony.*" The intimation was that any unsound, ugly, or unstable Thoroughbred mare—even one that had been rejected by "big horse" breeders—would be suitable for my stallion, and might even be an improvement. No matter that he had been imported, was bred from a family of superior performers, had a very respectable show record, some good offspring on the ground, and was the nick I'd sought for years for our foundation mare. To these breeders, he was still "only a pony."

Unfortunately, this attitude is not uncommon, and numerous ponies do end up being bred with no real plan in mind and no real attention paid to their ability to pass on superior conformation, soundness, sanity, athleticism, or heritage to their resulting foals. All of these are necessary qualities for a salable sporting animal. Yet all too often we hear people say that they became breeders because Old Flossie had been outgrown, and nobody could bear to part with her. Or because they thought that having foals around would be a fun educational experience for their children. Equally naive are those who, having seen the enormous price tags attached to successful pony hunters, believe that breeding ponies is the key to early retirement on a small fortune. Often the defense for ill-considered actions is that "ponies are pretty cheap, so we're not too much out of pocket, and anyway, you can always find a home for a cute pony."

This is true, but what kind of home will it be?

The "Now I want it/Now I'm tired of it" tendency that is rife in our society is not kind to domestic pets, as people at any animal shelter can tell you. Now that we've become largely a nation of urbanites or suburbanites with no relatives left on a family farm to educate us about the needs and responsibilities inherent in caring for larger animals, a frightening trend of treating horses and ponies with a casual "throwaway" attitude has grown up alongside that which already existed for dogs and cats. The countryside is littered with the sad offspring of accidental, uninformed, or poorly thought-out breedings of ponies. A visit to local auctions of animals whose formerly enthusiastic breeders have lost interest or gone bust, or to the sad barns of a hundred summer camps, or to the neglected ponies tied in the bare backyards of a thousand homes, is sobering. Although we've come a long way since the days when you could order a Shetland from the Sears catalogue complete with tack and in your choice of colors, the carelessness that has frequently been attached to the care and breeding of ponies is as heartbreaking as it is unnecessary.

I have written this book for several reasons. My primary purpose is to champion the pony breeds and share the love and respect that I (and many others like me) bear for the remarkably resilient qualities that have given them their unique and enduring characteristics. I also wish to illustrate the need to preserve these qualities, and to see the pony breeds taking their rightful place as a recognizable force in the greater realm of the breeding industry. And finally, I wanted to provide a clear, sensible, and practical guide for pony breeders (and prospective breeders) that can serve as a useful tool in the process of setting up a breeding operation, be it for the market or as a fulfilling hobby. This is the book I wish had existed when I began breeding ponies. I hope it meets its goals for you, and that it will provide you with the knowledge you need to start your own program.

Chapter

1

SO YOU WANT TO
BREED PONIES?

Those of us who are overwhelmed by the desire to "breed a few nice ponies" must realize that we are undertaking a serious business. While at first glance it may seem silly, the primary question to ask ourselves at the outset is actually a moral one: Are we willing to be responsible for filling the world with yet more ponies? Does the world actually *need* these ponies, and will there be a place for them? We all dream that *ours* (being more special than the norm) will find fond and caring homes where they will live out their lives in useful contentment; but it's a sad reality that a certain number may go for meat, or be ridden or starved to death by an ignorant sixth or seventh owner whose existence we'd rather not think about.

To pretend that this can't or won't happen is idealistic. To breed ponies without acknowledging their potential fate is irresponsible. As a sad example, I recall a phone call I made many years ago to try to find a man who for years had raised a large number of ponies from irreplaceable and immensely valuable imported stock. I already knew that this particular person had in turn gotten his ponies from another large importer whose huge herd had been dispersed piecemeal when the ponies did not prove to be as popular and successful a marketing venture as

1

Every pony breeder's dream: A rolling field full of beautiful mares and youngstock in an idyllic moment.

hoped. I discovered to my despair that all the ponies I was interested in had likewise been scattered to the four winds by their second owner, and that some priceless foundation mares had been sent to the killers in a desperate move to cut down on numbers even though they were neither old nor unsound. It was yet another instance of enthusiasm and optimistic ignorance gaining the upper hand over common sense. The ponies—and in a larger sense, the future generations of the breed involved—were the ultimate losers.

This story is, unfortunately, far from being an isolated case. And it leads us to a second critical question: Can we *afford* to breed ponies? Most of those experienced in the field agree that pony breeding is an expensive business that is neither for the weak of stomach nor the uneducated. More often than not it threatens to bankrupt even the most knowledgeable and dedicated horseperson. Rather than being a simple matter of putting Mare A in with Stallion B and waiting for nature to take its course, breeding even one mare can be a time-consuming and costly proposition. Taking the basic cost of caring properly for one pony per year, the potential breeder is immediately faced with stud fees (which can range from $500 to $1,500), mare care (hard to find at less than $10 a day), and vetting costs that include uterine cultures, biopsies, and ultrasound, and can extend to drugs to bring the mare into heat, take her out of it, cause her to ovulate, or keep her pregnant. This can run into the hundreds (sometimes thousands) of dollars. In the second half of her pregnancy, your mare will need more food and care. And all of this is incurred before the foal is even born.

From this point, pony breeding becomes a simple question of population. Breed five mares for three years in a row and in the fourth year you've gone from five to twenty mouths to feed, bodies to vaccinate and deworm, and feet to trim. We won't even *think* of the cost of insurance or the strain put on acreage that might have been minimal to begin with. And yes, this does take into account the fact that ponies are in general cheaper to keep as well as being hardier and healthier than most horses.

You might, of course, sell a few young ponies in the interim, but you're just as likely to have to hold onto your youngsters until they're of an age to do something under saddle, at which point the cost of training kicks in. Meanwhile, there are fences to repair, sheds to build, hay to buy when the region unexpectedly suffers a drought, and equipment (both mechanical and tack-related) to replace. It's the nature of the business that there will be culls that you wish had never been born as well as unexpectedly pleasant surprises. There are always vet bills when you can least afford them. The market for what you're breeding may be glutted just as your first two foal crops are of marketable age. Your chosen breed may not be well enough known in your area to have developed a sales niche. And there could be a recession. The occasional big-ticket sale suddenly looks like a drop in the bucket when outfaced by these and other farm expenses.

THE GOOD NEWS AND HOW TO KEEP IT THAT WAY

If you have innate good sense, you may find yourself beginning to agree with many professionals who maintain that buying ponies at the sales to school and sell is a lot cheaper than breeding and raising them at home. At least then *somebody else* is losing money. You may even be asking yourself whether breeding ponies is really such a good idea after all, and be content with the fun of producing a nice replacement for your good mare before retiring gracefully from the fray.

Yet there are perfectly sound reasons to breed ponies if that's what you dream of doing. Perhaps the outgrown mare has been such an exceptional performer and has such great conformation that you want to "clone" her for the benefit of future generations. This could be said to come under the heading of breeding "replacement stock," which in its larger form (in, for instance, the dairy cattle industry) provides an established and

Ponies have the nature, build, and talent to be adaptable to almost every conceivable job from child's best friend to a safe introduction to the showring, as Rachel Bertsche is finding on her Welsh cross. *Photo: Stan Phaneuf.*

Advancement through the highest junior levels of shows, Pony Club, or eventing are well within reach of many ponies with ambitious riders like Alexandra Putnam on Connemara Cybatina Lia (Fox Ridge Star light x *Amber Light). *Photo: Stan Phaneuf.*

legitimate business with a clear market focus. Perhaps you've fallen in love with a certain breed or an individual within that breed, and see a role that you can play by producing more of it for a specific segment of the pony-buying population. Maybe you consider evenings spent with your nose in a recent volume of a foreign studbook and the gambler's rush of genetics in theory versus genetics on the hoof too exciting to turn your back on. Possibly it's breeding the perfect show or combined driving pony that's your primary motivator; or maybe you simply want to breed the kind of ponies that you and your family (whether children or grown) will be able to enjoy riding and driving for many years to come. Even if all you're looking for is a hobby that will pay at least a good portion of its own bills, it pays to be clear about your motives.

Whatever the reason for starting, nearly every breeder who has stuck with a program for any number of years will agree that his or her success and longevity in the business has been due to

An athletic ability that far outstrips their size makes ponies equally suitable for adults with competitive goals, as illustrated by Connemara Captain Cricket (*Jiminey Cricket x LeWa's Lady of the Lake) with Linda Ellis. *Photo: Connemara Country File.*

the strict adherence to a certain set of characteristics that are hallmarks of nearly all pony breeds: temperament (and along with it, kindliness and a willing attitude), hardiness, versatility, conformation, intelligence, and marketability (which is sometimes a function of rarity).

Marketability is, of course, a necessity for anybody who wants to breed any kind of animal. The other traits (besides being essential attributes to most native pony breeds) have proven themselves invaluable to handlers who are often women or children of various ages and capacities, and who absolutely must have animals that are tractable on a daily basis, in the breeding shed, and in competition.

Thus it is that one Welsh breeder, in the business for nearly thirty years, can say that she began because the ponies were "beautiful, intelligent, and kindly. I also liked how versatile the breed was, and the variety of size." A prominent breeder of

Their presence at the highest levels of combined driving is well attested to by enthusiastic drivers. Here, Welsh cross Sky Line Drive and whip A. Sandra Davis are pictured en route to winning the Advanced Single Pony division at Fair Hill CDE, 1994. *Photo: Marion Poynter.*

Norwegian Fjords says, "We wanted to be sure that we could handle this breed in all situations—for example, handling the stallion during breeding. They have more than fulfilled our expectations." And a Connemara breeder of nearly forty years adds that after two decades of producing tractable and athletic ponies for a family of five children to ride, hunt, Pony Club, show, and that she could handle easily, she has continued on "because it has been so rewarding to make available such delightful ponies that bring enjoyment and success in every discipline; and in particular are ideal family ponies."

Comments like these make obvious the fact that just because it is serious business, it does not mean breeding ponies can't be fun. Negative messages and cautionary tales notwithstanding, it can be; and the statements above are typical of those heard from countless breeders who have found their ponies to be a continuous source of pleasure and satisfaction. Many prominent pony breeders who began because they had large families to mount have continued for a generation or more after the children grew up simply for love of the pony, a fascination with the process, and the conviction that their chosen ponies "still possess the qualities of conformation and willingness to do what we wanted"—this from a breeder who began in 1928! Not many have gotten rich from it in the financial sense. But nearly all agree that the satisfaction of seeing a homebred pony do well with a new and loving owner is impossible to measure.

You must, however, be absolutely realistic in your assessment of your expectations, the needs of the marketplace, and your ability to wait out the inevitable bad times when they occur. And it can't hurt to have the soul of a riverboat gambler, a steady job or a tidy independence, and a lot of pasture in a geographical area where the market is neither glutted nor nonexistent.

If your love for a certain breed demands that you dive into producing more of it, and you're willing to do the homework and put up with the strange hours, the expense, and the ever-changing popular opinion that drives the market, then take a deep breath and go ahead. You may find like the rest of us that the joy and challenge of raising the kind of ponies you've always dreamed of riding and driving will far outweigh any of the problems that crop up along the road.

Chapter

2

WHAT EXACTLY *IS* A PONY?

The established rules of the American Horse Shows Association, Canadian Equestrian Federation, and the governing bodies of most European countries codify the tradition that a pony is any equine not exceeding a maximum height of 14.2 hands (variously stated as 58 inches or 1.48 meters, depending on where you are) when fully mature. This arbitrary distinction creates a concrete and measurable dividing point between what constitutes a horse and what constitutes a pony, thus answering numerous thorny questions as to where the fine lines occur and who is eligible for what in the showring.

The result, of course, is that almost any breed contains individuals that are "official ponies" due to both environmental and heritable factors, especially those breeds whose average size straddles the thin line between "regulation" ponies and horses. There are thus numerous Morgan, Arabian, and Quarter Horse "ponies"; and the Thoroughbred "ponies" that appear from time to time are often highly popular in the showring and as producers of more refined crossbred hunter ponies.

Conversely, there are several pony breeds such as Connemaras and Welsh Section D Cobs whose marginal sizes regularly blend into the horse category, yet are still categorized as pony breeds. But to call a 14-hand Haflinger or Fjord a pony is to

9

risk a scathing retort from those who consider them small horses. The whole conundrum seems designed to cause nothing but confusion to those who attempt to answer arcane questions like, "When does a pony stop being a pony and start being a horse?"; "When does a horse become a pony?"; or "Is it still really a small horse?"

Some people will argue that size must be the final arbiter, in that horses and ponies share the same numbers of chromosomes and therefore spring from the same source. An experienced pony watcher will point out, however, that whereas a pony grown to horse size may lose a good percentage of the characteristics that give it its "pony look" and make it more "horsy" (i.e., longer heads and limbs, more refinement of bone, sparser manes and tails, etc.), horses that are shorter than the norm for their breeds do not suddenly develop traditional pony qualities along with smaller stature. This would seem to indicate that small horses are just that, while overgrown ponies are displaying certain traits of the horses that lurk in the nether generations of their pedigrees, of which size is only one heritable factor.

In most of Europe and the British Isles, this dilemma is solved by the simple refusal to register any member of a pony breed that grows "oversize" (except in the case of Welsh Section D Cobs, which have no upper height limit), a fate that doesn't seem to be shared by "undersized" members of recognized horse breeds.

North American breeders respond that pony breeds are still distinct, even when overgrown; that growth is an environmental factor achieved through better feed and care; and that therefore ponies outgrowing traditional height limits should not be penalized by exclusion from their breed registries if they meet all other standards. This is certainly valid, in that any animal that is a typical member of its breed should be stamped with a "look" that leaves little doubt as to what it is, regardless of its size. But it doesn't answer the question of what to do with those members of a breed that demonstrably lose type as they gain height, to become horses in everything but breed name.

Some people have suggested that a meaningful distinction between horses and ponies may exist in metabolism. Those who uphold this idea in the practical sense (i.e., years of observation and dealings with numerous horses and ponies of every shape, size, and description) maintain that ponies, as a whole, require less feed to maintain good flesh and condition, less energy to keep them warm, less effort to maintain healthy feet and constitution, more exercise to get them fit, and less effort to keep them that way than a horse of the same general make. This indication of pony metabolisms being generally slower than those of horses would explain their reputation for being easy keepers, as well as being a partial reason for some of their other unique characteristics.

Nearly every person who has dealt with ponies extensively will also have something to add about the pony's legendary intelligence, self-reliance, and advanced sense of humor. To those who love them, this only adds to their value in a pleasurable or competitive partnership.

For this discussion, however, I'm going to rely on the historical standpoint, which upholds the existence over many centuries of a number of breeds of small, tough animals that have evolved into their current forms from the ancient Celtic pony.

A BRIEF HISTORY OF THE DEVELOPMENT OF PONY BREEDS

Ponies have developed along very different lines from horses, even from ancient times. Nearly all of the pony breeds that we know today can be said with fair accuracy to have derived from a primitive type of animal that evolved from various even earlier primal migratory equids into a small, rugged, short-legged, rough-coated animal capable of living along the fringes of the harsh, moist, and mountainous coastal lands of western Europe and the British Isles with a minimum of human interference. This is the ancestor now commonly referred to as the Celtic pony. Small ears, hard, flinty feet, thick, oily manes, tails, and coats, broad jaws, short heads, and a constitution and metabolism built

11

to subsist on rough or sparse feed all had their part in an adaptation to the rigors of living in this kind of intractable climate and terrain. In fact, all of the major pony breeds that we know today developed their further specific breed characteristics in an environment very little changed from the one described.

It's thought that the modern Exmoor pony forms the closest and most ancient link with the Celtic pony, both in its skeletal makeup (especially that of the jawbone) and in the particulars of its color, markings, conformation, and the peculiar wind and water resistance of its coat, mane, and tail. Other breeds formed individual characteristics according to the specific elements to which they were exposed early on. These of course included periodic infusions of blood from Arabs, Barbs, Andalusians (or Spanish Jennets or Ginêtes, exceptionally beautiful and sought-after horses of easy gaits), Friesians, Scandinavian, and any other of the very ancient breeds that might have been expected to mingle with the equally ancient native (or indigenous) pony through movements of human population migration, trade, or war.

Human interference would have shown itself in the deliberate introduction of blood that would create an animal with the capacity to carry or pull heavy loads, to cover great distances at a trot over indifferent roads, to gallop tirelessly over uneven country without falling, to jump anything in its way, or any combination of the above, depending upon the current need. And of course this interbreeding would have been a two-way street, with the native pony being likewise put to incoming stock to improve the constitution, agility, temper, and staying ability of these sometimes more elegant animals.

Over time, the result of such additions would lead to the early development of modern horse breeds such as the Thoroughbred, Cleveland Bay, Irish Draught, the various European warmbloods, and so on. In the case of the pony (still relegated to the less arable and much rougher fringes of hill and coastline), the result of such crossings would have been honed and severely culled by natural laws of selection that favored the survival of those offspring closest to the prevailing native type, i.e., smaller, tougher, hardier, thriftier, more clever, and more agile.

A young Connemara stallion in a landscape very typical of that which is home to most native ponies.

This combination of genetics and environment, when occurring in those pockets of relative geographical isolation that encouraged a greater degree of inbreeding within an established population, provided an ideal setting for the evolution of the physical appearance of each region's ponies along increasingly specific lines. The inevitable effects of interbreeding and inbreeding resulted in a certain set of dominant characteristics being fixed in animals of a uniform type that would breed consistently true to that type. There was certainly a point in time when nearly every region of Europe boasted its own particular breed of pony as an end product of this evolution. By the nineteenth century, however, many of these had already begun to die out due to the effects of further outcrossing. But in the British Isles alone there still remained nine distinct native breeds of pony.

The shape and configuration of the Exmoor's skull is almost identical to prehistoric remains discovered in many parts of the Northern Hemisphere. The ability to adapt to severe climatic conditions, rough feed, and a harsh environment have caused its evolution into a pony of remarkable constitutional and genetic health; traits shared by most natives that have not been meddled with too greatly by humans in an effort to overrefine. *Photo: Anne Holmes.*

That these have maintained distinct and valuable characteristics despite generations of experimental or careless breeding is as much a tribute to the survival of certain dominant genetic characteristics as it is to the biological imperative of continued adaptation to a harsh environment. Even the famous even temperament and buoyant attitude of these ponies was doubtless formed over the same dozens of generations spent sharing intimately in the sparse lives and livelihoods of the people to whom they were partner as they developed. Ponies of uncertain temper, or that were in any way unwilling to perform the work required of them with anything less than cheerful compliance, were culled as ruthlessly by humans as the genetically unsound were by nature.

Temperament doesn't leave any trace except in the folklore of a people. But archeological findings of equine skeletal remains dating from thousands of years B.C. throughout the Northern Hemisphere do uphold the resemblance of modern ponies to these ancestors, and so the enduring Mountain and Moorland breeds we now know can rightly be said to have existed in some identifiable form "since time immemorial."

The Nineteenth Century

During the nineteenth century, the reigning British predilection for Arabs, Thoroughbreds, and Hackneys (the supreme road horse of the nineteenth century, and actually a blanket title used to differentiate the great trotting breeds and "roadsters" from common utility horses) led to a large number of these animals being crossed with native populations to "improve" them. This zealous if largely inefficient effort to refine the indigenous pony coexisted with a fever for meddling that accompanied the publication of Darwin's *The Origin of Species*. There were some successes, as witnessed by the modern Welsh Cob's strong trotting background and the Welsh pony's ability to absorb this trotting blood into its enduring gene pool with outstanding results.

An ill-conceived attempt to use Hackneys and even Clydesdales on some Connemaras, however, produced animals of such poor constitution that Irish smallholders refused to work with them or to breed from the few that were able to survive their intractable climate and impoverished lifestyle. The odd Thoroughbred or Barb seemed better suited to survival in mountainous coastal locales, although it may be that in the milder and more fertile interior, the draft and Hackney crosses aided in the early development of the modern Irish Draft.

Fortunately, the era just before the turn of the century brought a flurry of recognition from leading natural scientists as well as well-heeled sporting riders and drivers who came to regard the incredible soundness, sense, strength, and sheer athletic prowess of the native ponies with something akin to awe. They began to realize that the pony could actually be used to improve the horse. This reversal in attitude led to pockets of dedicated people finally banding together around their championed breeds to preserve what they now recognized as genetically superior qualities of soundness and constitution that, if lost, might prove to be an immeasurable and irreplaceable blow to the breeding of sound, adaptable, and intelligent horses suitable for the many different purposes of that day.

At that time, this still meant "utility"—whether working deep in the coal pits (where ponies replaced small children!); or as army remounts, packers, and artillery horses; or as the strong trotting "vanners" that served both the trades and the needs of any middle class family for reliable transportation. For those who could afford them, native ponies also served as a useful foundation for small ladies' hacks, durable hunters, and athletic polo ponies.

EARLY BREED SOCIETIES

The first organization developed to protect and promote a native breed was the Shetland Pony Stud Book Society, begun in 1890 when the pony population of the Shetland Islands was being decimated by a huge British and European demand for pit ponies. Nine years later, the Polo and Riding Pony Society of Britain opened sections for natives, and began to inspect and register them with the like goal of preserving their qualities, promoting an adherence to specific breed standards, and safeguarding their future development. In 1901, a separate Welsh Pony and Cob Society was born, and the Cuman Lucht Capaillini Chonamara (Connemara Pony Breeders Society of Ireland) followed suit in 1923.

The care and foresight of these groups has proven them to be a wise investment of time, labor, and money many times over. Especially in the most recent dark years between World Wars I and II, which saw the rapid obsolescence of all of the traditional uses horses and ponies had been maintained for, the breed societies and the people who upheld them kept small breeding herds of ponies from becoming either extinct or irremediably mongrelized. To keep farmers producing good ponies, the societies offered incentives, cash premiums, and competitive showcases. And when a vast new market of recreational riders, drivers, and pony-crazy children arose to make ponies popular again, the ponies were thankfully still there to fill the need.

ROMANCE AND REALITY

All pony breeds have histories steeped in romance and legend. This makes for great reading, as well as adding to the sense of historical value that you get when owning a pony from such an ancient heritage. It's fun to contemplate the idea, for instance, that the Connemara and the Shetland owe much of their heritage to Spanish horses shipwrecked on Irish and Shetland shores when the Spanish Armada sank in the sixteenth century. No matter that it's probably just as true (in the Irish case, anyway) that a proto-Andalusian element had already been introduced hundreds of years earlier by unromantic traders who included high-priced Spanish Jennets among their cargo. The Shetland, for its part, probably owes just as much to an influence of proto-typical Norwegian Fjords that arrived in the islands with the ancient Vikings. It's likewise lovely to think of Julius Caesar improving the quality of his Iberian war horses by crossing them with the courageous, intelligent, fast, and agile hill ponies of what is now Wales, which he admired greatly in their capacity as chariot ponies of the Britons he eventually conquered. In fact, if one reads history at all, the supremacy and nobility of the smart, tough, high-couraged British and Irish ponies is something that is alluded to with a great deal of regularity by most of the conquerors who lived and died by the quality and durability of their horses.

Relying on these mixed antecedents as a sole source of information about a breed, however, is about as useful as leaning too heavily on the modern Thoroughbred's connection with the combination of Arabians and native British mares (also largely Celtic pony-derived and probably including the influences of Welsh, Exmoor, and Connemara ponies) that spawned it. The link is certainly there but it's really the last seventy-five to one hundred years—or the period of time that has elapsed since the institution of breed societies and breed standards—that are the most useful when learning about the major pony breeds and their natures.

THE COMMON BREEDS

It would be impossible to describe every pony breed currently available in North America in detail within the space available here. While in no way complete, the following descriptions of popular breeds do serve to present an accurate view of those most commonly seen in the greatest variety of equine sporting disciplines, and that have earned a large following. This isn't to say that other breeds, given the chance, can't be just as successful or as popular. In fact, we hope that they will all become better known and appreciated as their obvious talents gain the recognition they deserve. A more complete listing of breed societies is included in the appendix and can give the reader access to other breeds both numerous and rare.

Meanwhile, the following is intended to help breeders and admirers of all ponies learn more about their own personal favorites while gaining insight into the broad range and abilities of some of the others and becoming aware of the similarities that unite them all.

Connemara

The Connemara pony has been ubiquitous on the rugged west coast of Ireland for many hundreds, and possibly even thousands, of years. In its native land it served as the family's beast of burden, plowing, hauling, and producing a foal every year to supply the family with some extra income or an eventual replacement for itself. On weekends, it was harnessed to the trap to take all to market or to Mass; and on holidays or festivals it would likely as not be unhooked to run in the "flaps" (races held on the beach) to bring home yet another badly needed infusion of cash. Cannonball, No. 1 in the Connemara Studbook and the most famous and sought after sire of his day, built his reputation as much on his undefeated record at the flaps over a twenty-year period as he did for his qualities as a sire.

In the nineteenth century, the breed began to attract a great deal of attention in England as an essential ingredient in the breeding of polo ponies and the famed Irish hunters, and large numbers of them were exported for that purpose. This newfound popularity, combined with a desperate need for income on the part of poor farmers in an era of extreme privation and political turmoil, led to the virtual denuding of Ireland's southern and western areas of its best ponies. Widespread and largely indiscriminate crossbreeding using everything from trotting Cobs to Barbs to Arabs to Hackneys to Clydesdales did nothing to help what was left, and at this point there were as many as five distinct types of Connemara pony on record.

A growing awareness of the need to preserve the original pony at home, and to encourage farmers to keep and breed from their best ponies rather than selling them off, led to the formation of the *Cuman Lucht Capaillini Chonamara* (Connemara Pony

Connemara stallion, Chiltern Colm (Corrib x Chiltern Gazelle). *Photo: Stan Phaneuf.*

Breeders Society) in 1923. The society instituted an ongoing program of inspections, registrations, and the purchase of likely colts. When grown, the best of these were sent out to stand in different parts of Connemara from where they would travel certain routes each week (frequently trotting beside their handlers' bicycles) to cover whatever mares awaited them at various crossroads.

This timely effort proved highly successful, but by the 1940s it became evident that some outside blood was needed to enlarge what has always been a small gene pool. During this period two Thoroughbreds, an Arab, and three Irish Draft stallions were used experimentally in a very limited fashion on native mares. The offspring that retained the best of the Connemara characteristics were kept from these crosses and duly registered. This led to the establishment of two new sire lines—one from the Connemara/Thoroughbred Carna Dun and one from the Connemara/Arab Clonkeehan Auratum. These joined the three native sire lines that had survived intact through the descendants of Connemara Boy, Rebel (a son of the aforementioned Cannonball), and Tully Lad (the only son of a pony called Mountain Lad) to form the basis of today's Connemara.

The first major importation of Connemaras to the United States occurred by the early 1950s, and the American Connemara Pony Society (ACPS) was established in 1956. In the decade following, the Connemara underwent a surge in popularity because of its superb temperament, soundness and sense, innate jumping ability, and an attendant size and stride that made it as desirable a ride for adults in the hunt field as it was for children in the showring or Pony Club rally.

The breed's current popularity is largely due to its continued fame as an all-rounder, not to mention the great successes of a number of individuals in the upper levels of combined training, an arena in which they frequently excel. Nearly as many can also be found in dressage, combined and pleasure driving, in the hunt field, as children's ponies, and as pleasure mounts. Some have also joined the ranks of winners in arenas as diverse as the hunter and jumper rings and competitive trail.

The Connemara is very popular as a superior cross for larger sporting horses, and in some cases has produced excellent crossbred pony hunters as well. The stud book has been closed to outside blood for more than thirty years, but the ACPS does maintain an active Halfbred Registry. As of 1995, the ACPS will begin a program of inspections for Connemaras being presented for registration in the society. The breed standard is as follows:

General   Connemaras are a product of their original environment: the rugged mountain coast of West Ireland. Sure-footed, hardy, and agile, they possess qualities of great stamina, staying power, and adaptability. They are renowned for their versatility and for their gentle, tractable, sensible, and willing disposition.

Temperament   Mannerly and manageable, kind, responsive, possessing good sense and basic intelligence.

Type   Rugged and sturdy; body compact, deep through the heart, with well-sprung ribcage and broad chest.

Action   Straight and true both front and rear with free movement in the shoulders and elbows; Connemaras should move underneath themselves in the rear and should be sure-footed, athletic, clever, and active, covering a lot of ground.

Head   Pony head of medium length with good width between large, dark, friendly eyes; well shaped with well-defined deep cheekbones, jaw relatively deep but not coarse, and head balanced in proportion to the rest of the body; neck of good length and definition, meeting the shoulder smoothly.

Shoulder   Long, well-laid back and with good slope.

Back   Strong and muscular. Some length of back is normal in Connemaras, especially mares, but should be well-ribbed up with strong loins.

Hindquarters   Well rounded and deep with good length from the point of the hip through the haunch; should balance the shoulders.

Bone   Clean, hard, flat, measuring seven to eight inches below the knee in ponies, more for horses; forearms and gaskins long and muscular, hocks strong and low set, cannons short and very dense.

21

Joints   Large and well defined.

Feet   Hard, strong.

Size   The most common range in the United States is from 13.3 hands to 15.0 hands, although occasional individuals may grow to 15.1 hands or 15.2 hands. It is sometimes felt that the larger ones may lose essential breed type. For this and other reasons, Connemaras are barred from registration in all other countries but the United States and Canada, when they grow over 14.2 hands.

Color   Predominantly grey, dun, bay, or brown; with occasional blacks, chestnuts, roans, palominos, and dark-eyed creams. Pintos are not allowed. Creams with blue eyes are barred from registration in other countries, but geldings and mares are allowed in the ACPS studbook in an appendix. The dark-eyed offspring of BEC mares are eligible for regular registration.

Haflinger

The Haflinger evolved from the small and rugged mountain horses of Austria's South Tyrol, and takes its name from the village of Hafling. The breed as it is known today originated in 1874 with the birth of the stallion 249 Folie, the result of a cross between the half-Arab stallion 133 El' Bedavi XXII, and a Haflinger mare of more than usual refinement. Although (as was common during this era) there were other horses of Oriental blood being used to refine the utilitarian mountain horse, it seems unlikely that they had any lasting influence. It was felt by breeders of the time that the offspring of these other outside stallions were lacking in the traits that they valued most in the Haflinger, and so after awhile their use ceased. 249 Folie thus became the founder and chief patriarch of the breed.

Seven stallion lines were eventually founded through this line in the form of the stallions 999 Anselmo, Bolzano, Massimo, Nibbio, Stelvio, 1074 Student, and 401 Liz. Willi. Male descendants of these lines all carry names beginning with the same letter of the alphabet as their forbear carried. Although in theory the same naming practice holds true for fillies, in fact it hasn't

The draft-type Haflinger Arcany (Amarquis x Coander).

necessarily carried throughout the generations; nevertheless, the Haflinger Association of America does now require that fillies' names start with the same first letter as their dams'.

In its native land, the Haflinger has long been valued as a thrifty, durable, and sure-footed animal equally suited to light draft, hauling, and packing while still having the quality to be an attractive pleasure driving animal and a suitable ride both on the trail and in competition. As such, they are equally popular as mounts for both adults and children. Stallions in Austria are all the property of the state, and are kept at government farms, a practice that is true for all horses and ponies bred there. Individual breeders keep their own mares and use the government stallions for their breeding programs. The resulting offspring are inspected before being accepted for registration.

As is so frequently the case, the breed suffered badly during the course of World Wars I and II, both through the high mortality of ponies used in the armed forces and through an immense loss of breeding stock, inaccurate record-keeping, and unintentionally careless breeding. The redrawing of borders that occurred in 1919 left the Tyrol divided between Austria and Italy, and had the side effect of bisecting what had been a largely harmonious breeding area. The broodmares were mostly quartered with their owners in South Tyrol (retained by Italy), but the best-quality government breeding stallions remained in Austria. Further difficulties that arose following World War II threatened to sink Haflinger breeding entirely, and it wasn't until the 1950s that the breed recovered and began to expand in numbers and popularity through the dedication and hard work of a handful of people.

Their labors thankfully proved very successful. Haflingers are now bred extensively throughout Europe, being especially popular in Germany, Switzerland, and Holland. The first members of the breed to come to the United States arrived in 1958 to take their place alongside of Tempel Farms' better-known Lippizzans. In their early days in this country, they were looked upon chiefly as a draft pony because of the breed's exceptional strength in relation to its size. Unfortunately, they were frequently referred to as "small Belgians" at this point, largely due to a similar chestnut coloring accompanied by a striking flaxen mane and tail. As such they became a common sight at fairs as pulling ponies and in draft hitches, two arenas that they still fill admirably. Their attractiveness and tractability has won them a widening circle of admirers in recent years, with the result that it's becoming more common to see them being ridden by children in 4-H, western pleasure, and the local hunter pony ranks. Adults are a part of the equation, too, using Haflingers variously as pleasure mounts, in lower-level dressage, at combined and pleasure driving competitions, and being enjoyed by a growing number of people as ideal family ponies with the brains and ability to serve many purposes.

The Haflinger Association of America (HAA) was established in 1976, and has kept up its ties with the World Haflinger

Association. This organization, located in Innsbruck, Austria, oversees around thirteen international member associations, and is instrumental in the preservation and continuation of breed type.

Increased popularity in North America has, of course, put pressure on breeders to produce Haflingers that are taller and more refined than the "draft type" that was common twenty years ago. While recognizing that both lighter and heavier types of ponies already occur in the breed, the HAA still recommends that any extremes of type be avoided, and that the breed's outstanding characteristics be maintained: "The overall impression should be of a small, powerful horse of unusual conformation and beauty with a friendly, intelligent expression and bearing of great vitality and eagerness." The breed standards are as follows:

Size Fifty-two to fifty-nine inches high (with stallions sometimes growing to sixty inches).

Head and Neck Small, flat or slightly dished and broad, with wide-spaced eyes and small ears. Neck strongly arched, with a full, thick mane that may be double, and heavy forelock.

Body Powerful and well sprung. Broad chest and rump, sometimes with double croup. Full tail. Sleek coat, solid or with dappling. Coarseness is *not* to be found in the Haflinger.

Limbs and Feet Strong, well-tapered legs with relatively large, hard hooves.

Movement Free and easy movement, with a long stride. Ponderous movement is *not* to be found in the Haflinger.

Color Chestnut body color, ranging from honey blond to chocolate. Tail and mane color varies from pure white to flaxen.

Norwegian Fjord

Excavations of Viking burial sites have given evidence that ancestors of the Norwegian Fjord have been bred for around two thousand years in western Norway. Besides being widely used for packing, hauling, and agricultural work, the early Fjords were also used in the dubious Viking sport of stallion fighting, and

Norwegian Fjord stallion, Gjest (Helgas-Jarl x Rita). *Photo: Richard Broadbent.*

they were almost certainly raised for meat in addition to all of these other purposes. Over the years, the latter two uses dwindled, and the Fjord evolved into Norway's chief all-purpose pony. It is invaluable as a light draft animal in areas that are too mountainous or rough for machinery, as well as serving as a superior packing and riding animal renowned for a steady temperament, hardy constitution, willing attitude, and surefootedness. In modern times it has grown very popular and is widely bred throughout Scandinavia and in Germany. Some of the best breeding stock in recent years has come from Denmark, where it has been particularly successful.

Believed to have descended from relatives of the primitive Przewalski's Horse as it migrated west from the Steppes, the

Fjord may in fact still be one of the purest of the native pony breeds. The relative isolation of its homeland, and the subsequent lack of outcrossing that has occurred because of this, has resulted in a breed that has had very little outside influence on its development and maintenance as an entity. The Norwegian Fjord Horse Registry continues to safeguard this purity by forbidding any form of crossbreeding using Fjords. In fact, stringent rules dictate that any stallion used on mares of other breeds will have its papers revoked. In this sense the Fjord can be said to stand more or less on its own as a breed, having neither influenced nor been influenced by any other breeds to an enormous extent. To its growing coterie of admirers, this is one of its chief attributes, although it has obviously led to very close breeding along the way. For instance, the "matador," or most influential founding father of the modern Fjord is generally considered to be Njal 166, born circa 1884, which contained three crosses to a pony called Gange-Rolv. Of the other major lines that have had a strong and lasting effect on breeding herds the world over— Baronen 193 (1894), Rosenkrantz 239 (1897), Bergfast 634 (1899), Hakon Jarl 645 (1913), and Oyarblakken 819 (1923)— only Baronen was not a son or grandson of Njal, but he also traced back to Gange-Rolv.

The Fjord retains the primitive pony's dun coloring. While this is common among many pony breeds, and not uncommon among some Spanish-derived breeds like the Quarter Horse and mustang, it isn't quite as specific or as widespread as it is to the Fjord, in which it is the only recognized color. It is often accompanied by an "eel" or dorsal stripe running the length of the spine from ears to tail, as well as by occasional zebra striping on the legs and across the withers. All these markings are hallmarks of the primitive ponies and horses of the Steppe, Forest, and Celtic variety from which the breed is descended. Further enhancing this interesting coloration is the fact that the Fjord's mane and tail grow with black hairs in the center, surrounded by cream or flaxen hairs on either side. The mane is traditionally trimmed in a crescent shape that accentuates an arched neck, with the cream hairs trimmed somewhat shorter so that the black stripe in the center is highly visible.

A few Fjords were imported to the United States in the last years of the nineteenth century. In 1906, one Warren Delano Roosevelt imported a stallion and six mares with the intent, so Fjord history tells us, of creating a "khaki colored mount for a khaki covered soldier." History doesn't relate why this artistic vision failed to come to fruition. Another influx of Fjord imports occurred in the 1950s, but it wasn't until the 1970s that ponies of real quality were imported and the breed gained a strong and lasting foothold in North America.

As is frequently the case with heavier breeds, the original ponies imported were used most frequently for utility, pulling, light farm work, trail riding, and packing. As the breed's reputation for intelligence, hardiness, and willingness grew, it became more common to see Fjords under saddle as suitable mounts for adults and teenagers alike. In their capacity as ideal driving ponies, they have become very popular at competitions where they excel in both pleasure and combined driving at all levels. The lighter ones have also proven themselves to be very respectable movers and jumpers, and can be seen competing successfully in dressage and over fences. The combination of size, temperament, ability, and hardiness makes the Fjord an excellent choice as a family pony, and it is in this role that they are frequently seen at their best.

The Norwegian Fjord Horse Registry still works in conjunction with its parent body in Norway to promote the continuation of traditional breed characteristics and the importance of good breeding practices. In addition to keeping records on registered animals and statistics on the breed in North America, it also hosts a Judges Training Program in conjunction with the Norwegian Society.

The breed standards are as follows:

Head and Neck   Should present an appearance of elegance without coarseness. Head medium sized and well defined with broad, flat forehead and a straight or slightly dished face. Eyes are large, ears small and alert. The neck is well muscled and crested.

Body   Short coupled, with good depth, large heart girth, and well-developed muscles.

Limbs and Feet The legs are powerful, with substantial bone and excellent feet that are black in color.

Size Between 13.2 hands and 15.0 hands, and weighs between nine hundred and fifteen hundred pounds.

Color Always dun, with no white markings. Ninety percent are brown dun, the remaining ponies are red, grey, pale, gold, or yellow duns. All have the distinctive black points and striping as mentioned above. In the case of red duns, these stripes will be reddish-brown in color; in greys, black or darker grey; in cream duns, red, brown, or black.

Shetland (American Type)

On its native islands, the Shetland was used time out of mind for general utility—packing, hauling, plowing, pulling, and even as a ridden conveyance by grown men whose feet must certainly have skimmed the ground when mounted. British visitors to the harsh landscape of the Shetland Islands in the nineteenth century were much taken with the strength, vitality, temperament, and beauty of these ponies, and a lot was written at that time about their hardiness and essential freedom from ailments and lameness, especially given the amount of work they were required to do in total disregard to their size. They were still seen as something of a novelty, however, until their role as a replacement for small children in the deeper and narrower coal tunnels of England became clear in the middle part of the century. Hundreds of animals were exported as pit ponies in that era; and it wasn't long after this that the Shetland Pony Stud Book was developed.

Shetlands were among the earliest ponies to be imported to North America, where they found a ready market from the 1880s on as children's ponies, mounts for the pony ride concessions that sprang up at almost every public event or recreational "paradise," and as the companions of numerous itinerant photographers who strolled through suburban neighborhoods with a comet's tail of entranced children all begging their mothers to accept the photographs so that they could sit on the pony. They were also popular as novelty acts in circuses, at fairs, and in parades, where they could be seen hitched to miniature versions of brewery wagons, vans, and a whole realm of commercial vehicles used for publicity purposes by all sorts of business enterprises. They continued to be valued for their immense strength in relationship to their diminutive size, and it wasn't long before their game trotting ability and competitive spirit made them just as popular as roadster and racing ponies. There was even a time in recent memory when you could order a Shetland pony in your choice of colors, complete with tack, from the Sears, Roebuck, and Company Catalog.

Many of these early ponies traced their heritage to such well-known native foundation sires as Prince of Thule, Lord of the Isles, and Jack. The desire for greater refinement and showring flash led to imported Shetlands being interbred with Hackney ponies to develop a taller, lighter, high-actioned Shetland of American (or "Modern") type that bears little resemblance to its British relatives. Not everybody applauded this tendency, however, and many regretted the loss of substance and temperament that has always marked the Shetland as a child's ideal first pony. In some areas there has been a resurgence in popularity of breeders who specifically concentrate on the Classic (or "Island") type Shetland—a type that is relatively free of outside blood and built more along the utilitarian lines that characterized the original breed. Many of these ponies trace back to such important foundation stallions as Colonel Cody, Hillsides Oracle, Silver Crescent, and King Larigo. The latter two proved especially potent and through their mutual grandson Silver King X, founded a dynasty that exists to this day. The American Shetland Pony Club has been able to find room for all types, and to provide competitive showcases for just about everything that can be done with them.

Modern Shetlands are as versatile as their ancestors were. Still the nonpareil of small children's ponies, their size, good-humored nature, and tolerance makes them ideally suited to their important job of teaching a future generation of horsepeople how to ride and care for a pony by themselves. Yet, like most pony breeds, their diminutive size carries with it the scope, strength-per-ounce, and athletic ability that has found a particular outlet for adults in the driven disciplines. In addition to their popularity as racing, roadster, and fine harness ponies, Shetlands outgrown by a family's youngest riders are equally adept as the family's pleasure driving pony. Many have also made a splash in timed events such as cones, obstacles, and scurry competitions, where their small size, agility, and quick intelligence can give them a certain advantage.

The Shetland has had a further role in the evolution of at least three prominent American pony breeds. Their effect on Chincoteague ponies is a matter of record. They also formed the foundation and backbone of the Miniature Horse, which in some circles has outstripped its forbear in popularity. And the Pony of the Americas, the end product of using a Shetland pony stallion on Appaloosa mares to create an all-round Western family type pony for children and teenagers, has grown to be a well-known and respected breed in its own right, to take its place with the other major pony breeds in all forms of ridden and driven

American Classic Shetland stallion Queen Ann's Jet (Duke's Royal Master x Rip's Queen Ann). *Photo: Pat Fisher Pawlowicz.*

competition for both adults and children. While each of these breeds has developed along distinct lines, each still owes a great deal of its substance, size, conformation, and temperament to the original Shetland foundation.

The American Shetland Pony Club itself was formed in 1888 (thus slightly predating the British Society!), and remains the largest pony registry in North America. It currently lists somewhere in the vicinity of seventy-five hundred members, and maintains extensive records on well over a hundred thousand ponies.

The general conformation of the American Shetland is described as follows:

General   Shetland conformation should be that of a strong, attractive, versatile pony, blending the original Shetland type with refinement and quality resulting from American care and selective breeding.

Body and Limbs   The barrel should be well rounded, back short and level, with flat croup. The pony shall have a full mane and tail; coat should be fine and glossy. The pony's structure should be strong with refinement; high withers; sloping shoulders; flat-boned, muscular legs (not cow- or sickle-hocked); strong, springy pasterns and good, strong serviceable feet.

Head and Neck   The head should be carried high and on a well-arched neck and should be symmetrical and proportionate to the body, with width between prominent eyes; a fine jaw; short, sharp, and erect ears; small muzzle, with flaring nostrils and a refined throatlatch.

Color   Besides the "normal" hard colors like black, bay, etc., Shetlands come in an array of lovely hues that include all manner of pintos as well as an assortment of unusual livers, chocolates, and silver dapples. Ponies may occasionally have blue eyes, which is not considered to be a fault.

Size   May not exceed 11.2 hands, or forty-six inches. Moderns are divided into divisions for ponies under forty-three inches and ponies forty-three inches to forty-six inches, with Classics generally somewhat smaller than Moderns.

The Welsh Pony and Cob

Like the other native breeds, the Welsh pony honed its genetic ability to adapt to hardship by being relegated for many hundreds of years to land that was too boggy to be healthful for sheep and too steep and stony to be easily cultivated. It's hardly an exaggeration to say that prototypes of today's ponies have inhabited the Welsh hills since before Roman times, and there exists plenty of written evidence of Henry VIII (already notorious for his ill treatment of numerous wives) and his attempts to exterminate all ponies under 14 hands. In subsequent generations the ponies were chased off of good grazing by landowners, shepherds, and dogs—at one point even being hunted for sport—as often as they were maintained and praised by those who appreciated their enduring qualities. Yet after all the abuse, it's hard to beat a Welsh pony for sheer beauty and gaiety, qualities that seem as much a part of the pony's basic character as they are of the varied early influences of Arab, Barb, Cob, and Hackney blood.

This combination of heritages led to the existence of distinct Arab type and Cob type Welsh by the nineteenth century, with the Cobs tending to be of greater size and bulk. The Welsh Pony and Cob Society studbook has thus been divided into four sections almost since the beginning, with the current divisions being established by 1949: Section A, for Welsh mountain ponies not exceeding 12.2 hands; Section B, for Welsh ponies of riding type not exceeding 14.2 hands; Section C, for Welsh ponies of Cob type not exceeding 13.2 hands; and Section D, for Welsh Cobs over 13.2 hands and with no upper height limit. In this way the vagaries and arguments created by differences of type and size have been largely eliminated, as long as the ponies concerned meet the standard of their respective sections.

The breed has always been blessed with a large number of extremely strong stallions. In early days, ponies such as Dyoll Starlight (unquestionably the most beautiful and influential pony of his day), Eiddwen Flyer III, Klondyke, Dick Hill, and Prince of Cardiff maintained an effect that can be felt to this day, frequently through the blood of the legendary Section A pony, Coed Coch Glyndwr. And there are few modern Section B Welsh that don't owe

Welsh Section A stallion, Barlys Troi of Penrhyn (Bengad Rochea x Ceulan Shoned).

Welsh Section B mare, Penrhyn China Belle (Carolinas Red Fox x Penrhyn Merry Chimes).

some part of their quality to that section's ancestors, Tan-Y-Bwlch Berwyn (often through his son Coed Coch Berwynfa) and Craven Cyrus. Coed Coch Glyndwr shows up again as another of the chief Section B ancestors, through his famous grandson Criban Victor.

Nearly all Section C and D Cobs trace back to the stallions Trotting Comet, True Briton, Alonzo the Brave, and Cymro Lwyd, with later descendants such as Eiddwen Flyer, Ceitho Welsh Comet, and Llanarth Braint taking their place as founders of their sections in due course. A student of pedigrees will find that the foundations of all four sections carry a tremendous amount of crisscrossing between sections, so that, for instance, the aforementioned Coed Coch Glyndwr might be influential in Sections A, B, *and* C, whereas a Section D founder like Eiddwen Flyer is also likely to appear in the back pedigree of many modern Section A's. This pattern of movement among sections still exists, although it's generally frowned on to breed too far from the source by mixing breeding stock from, say, Sections A and D.

The Welsh studbook was closed to further infusions of Cob, Hackney, Barb, or Arab breeding by the 1930s, and by 1960 it was additionally closed to ponies of unregistered parentage that had previously been allowed registration on inspection in order to broaden the breed's base.

Welsh of all descriptions began to make their way to the United States by the 1880s, and the Welsh Pony and Cob Society of America was founded in 1907, only a few years after that of its parent organization. After some years of fluctuating fortunes that were largely driven by World Wars I and II and an intervening Depression, the ponies began to boom in popularity in the 1950s, a position that has shown little sign of abating. In many circles the Section A and B ponies are consistently considered to be the premier children's pony in all disciplines imaginable, as well as serving as a good foundation from which to produce winning crossbred hunter ponies for the showring. For adults they are a superior driving pony. There are numerous opportunities for showing them in Breed competition both in hand, under saddle, and in harness, and they are omnipresent at every level of competition from 4-H to the AHSA "A" show circuit. They have also

Welsh Section C stallion Turkdean Sword Dance, pictured at twenty-seven years (Turkdean Cerdin x Llanarth Dancing Satellite).

lived up to their hard-trotting ancestry by serving as successful trotting ponies in areas where these are in demand for racing.

The Welsh Cobs, while less numerous and perhaps not as widely known in North America, have proven equally adaptable to all phases of equine endeavor. The larger Section D's are superior all-rounders that frequently make topnotch driving ponies and horses, and that are also seen in increasing numbers competing in dressage and over fences. Their size, attractiveness, scope, and boldness make them ideal mounts for both teenagers and adults, who find them well able to hold their own in open competition in any discipline. The same can be said of the smaller Section C Cobs, which (besides their strengths in harness) are also generally well up to the weight of a small adult whether the object is pleasure, hunting, or combined training. Cobs have also

Welsh Section D stallion Llanarth Trustful (Derwyn Telynor x Llanarth Sian). *Photo: Bunny Ramsay.*

made their mark in the production of wonderful halfbred sport horses suitable for all disciplines.

The standard for the Welsh pony is as follows:

General Character   Hardy, spirited, and ponylike.

Color   Any color except piebald and skewbald.

Head   Small, clean cut, well set on, and tapering to the muzzle.

Eyes   Bold.

Ears   Well placed, small and pointed, well up on the head, proportionately close.

Nostrils   Prominent and open.

Jaws and Throat   Clean and finely cut, with ample room at the angle of the jaw.

Neck   Lengthy, well-carried, and moderately lean in the case of mares, but inclined to be cresty in the case of matured stallions.

Shoulders   Long and sloping well back. Withers moderately fine but not "knifey." The humerus upright so that the foreleg is not set in under the body.

Forelegs   Set square and true, and not tied in at the elbows. Long strong forearm, well-developed knee, short flat bone below knee, pasterns of proportionate slope and length, feet well shaped and round, hooves dense.

Back and Loins   Muscular, strong, and well coupled.

Girth   Deep.

Ribs   Well sprung.

Hindquarters   Lengthy and fine. Not cobby, ragged, or goose-rumped. Tail set well on and carried gaily.

Hindlegs   Hocks to be large, flat and clean with points prominent to turn neither inwards nor outwards. The hindleg not to be too bent. The hock to be set behind a line from the point of the quarter to the fetlock joint. Pasterns of proportionate slope and length. Feet well shaped, hooves dense.

Action   Quick, free, straight from the shoulder, well away in front. Hocks well flexed with straight and powerful leverage and well under the body.

The standards for the Welsh pony of Cob type (Section C) and the Welsh Section D Cob differ in some, though by no means all respects, and are as follows:

General Character   Strong, hardy, and active, with pony character and as much substance as possible.

Color   As above.

Head   Full of quality and pony character. A coarse head and Roman nose is most objectionable.

Eyes   Bold, prominent, and set widely apart.

Ears   Neat and well set.

Neck   As above.

Shoulders   Strong, but well laid back.

Forelegs   As above. Also, when in the rough, a moderate quantity of silky feather is not objected to but coarse, wiry hair is a definite objection.

Middlepiece   Back and loins muscular, strong, and well coupled. Deep through the heart and well ribbed up.

Hindquarters   Lengthy and strong. Ragged or droopy quarters are objectionable. Tail well set on.

Hindlegs   As above.

Action   Free, true, and forcible. The knee should be bent and the whole foreleg should be extended straight from the shoulder and as far forward as possible in the trot. Hocks flexed under the body with straight and powerful leverage.

The Crossbred Conundrum

Many of the best ponies being bred for the showring today are crosses between two or even three different breeds, and thus to describe them as a unit is less a question of trying to compare apples and oranges as it is one of apples and avocados. In essence, the breeding of crosses is an equine equivalent of "building the better mousetrap." The crosses that work most consistently well are largely dependent on the job the ponies are expected to do, the average skill, size, and age of the adults or children to whom the breeder expects to sell them, and the perceived need of a market for a certain type of pony that cannot adequately be filled by one of the various fullbreds that are available.

A case in point here is the pony hunter market. At top-rated shows in North America, a pony hunter must fulfill several very tough criteria. First and foremost, it must be an impeccable mover. In this context, there is no room for a pony that is short in its stride, or that is a little too round in its trotting action. What's wanted is a daisy cutting style of long, low action that gives the appearance of skimming lightly over the ground. Next, it must be both pretty and loaded with quality and refinement. Small pony hunters can get away with looking more ponylike, but the large pony hunters are expected to look as nearly as possible like small horses (or more specifically, Thoroughbreds). To succeed in either section, the individual must be able to jump in good form (something most ponies do naturally), and it should have at least a moderately kind temperament, although this frequently takes a back seat to the other characteristics.

Most fullbred native ponies don't have the absolute quality, refinement, and movement required of hunter ponies that will go to the top in AHSA-rated competition. In order to achieve these things, crossing native ponies with a more refined small horse with impeccable conformation and movement is necessary. The

Hidden Creek's Rainfox (by the legendary Welsh sire, Cymraeg Rainbeau x the well bred Thoroughbred Thomirror) typifies the superior results that can be achieved in careful crossbred programs capable of producing show hunter ponies of the highest caliber. *Photo: Ed Keller.*

most popular cross for the hunter pony ranks is thus the Welsh/Thoroughbred, although there are a certain number of Shetland crosses, a few Arabs, some Connemaras, and the odd Quarter Horse. For driving, crosses designed to produce a more refined or sometimes scopier pony may cover all of these crosses as well as including some Morgans.

Breed type is not as critical as it is in a fullbred program. As one well known breeder puts it, "I do not look for breed type in crossbred stock, nor do I look at bloodlines, as I do not consider crossbred stock as a gene pool that will go on and on. I consider crossbreds as usually a one- or two-generation product. The good ones seem to be lost to the performance world as soon as they enter it." Thus it is that if you have a mare or stallion that is very well made and bred but too refined to be thought of as a good example of its breed type, it could be an ideal foundation for a crossbred program. This assumes, of course, that the individual combines refinement with superior movement, temperament, and the best constitutional attributes of its breed. If it's simply a weed, it isn't a good breeding prospect. Period.

Crossbreeding owes its success to "hybrid vigor." This genetic term basically means that the offspring of two unrelated parents may be much better than either parent. Nobody understands exactly why hybrid vigor works the way it does. The general idea is that, by introducing a wider variety of genetic material than that which characterizes a specific breed or individual, you enlarge the capacity for that material to combine in ways that maximize the resulting offspring's ability to excel in certain venues. Crossbreds may thus be smarter, more agile, better built for a broad array of purposes, sounder, and healthier than their parents.

The problem with hybrid vigor is that, because of the variety of genetic material available, it won't generally "breed true" in the next generation. Say you have a Welsh/Thoroughbred mare that is really superb in conformation, temperament, and ability. You breed her to a Welsh/Thoroughbred stallion of equal quality, thinking to double your blessings. This might occur, if you're lucky. But the chances are better that you'll get something that isn't quite as good as either of its parents. You may get a weedy pony with big feet, or a horse whose legs are proportionately too short for its big body. You may get a horsy head on a pony body, a pony's rounder movement on a horse's lankier frame, a tendency to lameness that you weren't expecting, or an awkward temperament that seems to come from out of nowhere. The combinations are as endlessly varied as the backgrounds of the ponies concerned.

For this reason, most experienced breeders recommend using two fullbreds to create a successful crossbreeding foundation. Then, if a third cross is desired, go back to the fullbred that most nearly approaches the qualities that you're trying to pass on. If, for instance, you start with Welsh mares and a Thoroughbred stallion, you may want to breed your Welsh/ Thoroughbred mares back to an outstanding Welsh stallion to maintain the pony size and qualities you're looking for.

This is not to say that a three-way breeding can't work. In the 1960s and 1970s, for instance, one noted Thoroughbred and pony breeder obtained a great measure of success using a celebrated imported Thoroughbred stallion that stood only 14.2 hands on imported mares of varied Welsh, Thoroughbred, and Arab breeding. The result in many cases was a hunter pony of immense attractiveness and considerable ability, with the long daisy cutting movement required to win the hack classes in big shows. This breeder concedes, however, that it didn't always work out as hoped. There were ponies that grew to be quite large horses, other ponies that reached that nether region ranging from 14.3 hands to 15.1 hands that is notoriously difficult to market for the showring, and ponies whose temperaments turned out to be completely unsuitable either for children or for the stresses of upper-level competition. When this happens, it isn't uncommon for a hot but otherwise exceptional mare to be bred back to a native pony of exceedingly kind nature and unflappable disposition to try to reinstate the necessary balance between glamorous looks and the disposition required to excel as mounts that are ostensibly safe for children.

Chapter

3

FINDING THE PERFECT PONY
FOR THE JOB

With no indigenous horse or pony breeds of its own, North America has traditionally been dependent on importing ponies from elsewhere to develop its own style of breeding. In time, it may be that feral pony-sized types like the Spanish mustang or the Chincoteague pony may ultimately join the Pony of the Americas as distinctly American pony breeds. Meanwhile, we continue to owe most of our pony heritage to the effects of the British Mountain and Moorland ponies, of which three—the Shetland, the Welsh, and the Connemara—have formed the backbone of North American breeding populations. Add to this the great numbers of crossbred ponies being produced specifically for the pony hunter market, and the current popularity in certain circles of heavier types like the Norwegian Fjord and the Austrian Haflinger, and you have a group that is notable in its variety.

At a breed show some years ago, a Welsh breeder was holding forth at great length about the "horrible" Connemara mare that had been awarded the day's breed championship in her division. Shocked, I asked her to elaborate, since I thought the animal a very nice example of a Connemara broodmare. The other breeder cited the mare's goose rump and too great a length from point of hip to hock as opposed to a Welsh's high tail carriage, level croup, and shorter gaskin. I remarked that I thought the mare had a strongly muscled, deep, sloping rump, and well let down hocks indicative of great jumping ability. (The ongoing tail carriage argument does, by the way, have an interesting historical note attached to it, to wit: The "gay" carriage of the Welsh and its relatives is thought by some to be directly attributable to a dominant Arab influence; the more sloping hindquarter and lower carriage of the Connemara and certain other breeds being a characteristic of the Barb.) She cited the Connemara mare's long back in relation to a Welsh's shorter and closer coupled one. I pointed out the breadth and depth of a body I thought perfect for carrying even large foals with ease. She cited the mare's plain head. I admitted that Connemaras are not always noted for their beautiful heads, but discovered that it wasn't the size the other breeder objected to, it was the fact that it wasn't short, dished, or wide enough between the eyes. And that the ears (perhaps a shade long, but nicely shaped and well set) didn't have that wonderful short, ultracocked and alert quality that one finds in a classic Welsh pony.

Having gotten this far, we agreed that we didn't know a great deal about the standards of each other's breeds, or why they were judged the way they were. We spent the rest of the evening very pleasantly discussing our breeds' traits in relation to the sort of work we did with them, and why they were important. We both came away understanding a lot more about pony type in general and breed type in particular.

Our discussion also brought home two points quite clearly. First, as suggested above, that although ponies may share some genetic similarities, they are anything but *generic*. They have adapted over many centuries to a broad range of climatic and forage-related conditions that have given them sets of characteristics that are absolutely specific to their breeds. And these need to be valued and protected at all costs.

Second, that if you're going to be successful in breeding a particular kind of pony, you'd better start by being absolutely certain of its breed characteristics, both good and bad. Once you've educated yourself thoroughly, you should be able to recognize your pony breed, even in halfbred form, wherever you go. And finally, *you must love your chosen pony as a type*. Its form and make should fill your eye—another way of saying that looking at it should give you pleasure.

It follows that whether you choose to breed Connemaras or Welsh Cobs or Dartmoors, they must fit their societies' breed standards, and those standards must describe an animal that you find attractive and useful. Otherwise, why bother? The variety of choices available makes it absurd not to choose a pony that you like looking at every morning and that is built to do what you want it to do.

No greater disservice can be done to a pony breed than to consider it merely an Arab or Thoroughbred or warmblood in a smaller package, rather than being a distinct and valuable entity in its own right. And if breeding animals like this is in fact your goal, good fullbreds that meet their breed standards can make a wonderful foundation for a halfbred program that has the potential of achieving the best of both worlds. This will make you much happier, in the long run, and you won't have spoiled a perfectly adequate pony breed in a frustrating and largely fruitless attempt to turn it into something it was never designed to be.

ASKING THE RIGHT QUESTIONS

The next series of questions to ask yourself begins with, *What is it that you want to breed for, and what niche do you see your ponies occupying?* What job is it that you think they'd be perfect for, and how does that fit in with your marketing and/or competitive goals? Whatever your focus, you need to know everything possible about the breeds and crosses involved, how they have worked in the past (or haven't), how they work now (or don't), how they hold up in your discipline, and, if they're crossbred, which sides the crosses are most effective in, and what the most successful percentages have been. Have your ponies' relatives gotten good press from the people in your area that ride and drive them? Do people wonder aloud where to find more like the ones that are out there performing so well? And if the local market is low or

Ponies are the quintessential all-rounders. Connemara mare Tower Hill's Leannan is seen here as breed champion. *Photo: Stan Phaneuf.*

She serves a turn as son's instructor.

She is also the family pleasure driving pony.

And she changes hats again to be mother's show pony. *Photo: Stan Phaneuf.*

glutted, is there a larger regional or national market for your chosen type of pony in the discipline that interests you most?

Next, *Who are the people you intend to have buy most of your ponies?* When you imagine where you'd like to be in five years, does your market niche consist mainly of family all-rounders, adult amateurs, children, riders, drivers, or a combination of all these categories? If you want to attract adult amateurs as well as children, one of the larger breeds whose tendency is to span the size range from medium pony to small horse might be your best bet, unless your chief interest is driving. If, on the other hand, you want to keep your market strictly focused on the needs of younger children, any of the smaller breeds and crosses may serve your purposes far better than one whose upper size limits can't be guaranteed with any certainty until they've grown to the embarrassing height of 14.2 1/2 hands or 14.3 hands.

Now, *What specific disciplines do you want to target?* Top-flight hunter ponies for the showring? Ponies that will excel at combined driving? All-rounders that will take their turn at the shows, in the hunt field, at some horse trials, and maybe drive as well? These are all purely personal decisions, grounded firmly within the parameters of your own areas of interest and expertise. If you love a specific pony breed because it already does what you want to do and is capable of reaching the levels you see as needing more solid campaigners for either children or adults like yourself, you're several steps ahead of the game.

You'll also need to take a good hard look at *What does your breed excel at realistically?* As mentioned above, the idea of trying to mold a pony breed into an image or role that we wish it to fit rather than that which it was designed for is an exercise in futility. To expect a breed not renowned for its quality of movement or length of stride to compete successfully in dressage or as a showring hunter against ponies bred specifically for those characteristics, for example, is frustrating and unfair to both yourself and the pony. You may, for instance, have lovely, typical ponies of a certain breed that do exceptionally well in hunter, dressage, or driving divisions at their respective breed shows up to the National level. They may still have trouble being looked at in open competition where they are pitted against a larger and

In defining your market niche, it's essential to be realistic about your breed's ability to fulfill your expectations. While a Shetland or Shetland cross will never be able to succeed as an adult amateur hunter, for example, they are perfect as a child's first pony from leadline through short stirrup, as shown by Miranda LeKacos on Peanut Butter and Jelly. *Photo: Stan Phaneuf.*

When outgrown, they can make wonderful driving ponies for adults, like Grandprix's Something Else (Queen Ann's Jet x Kewpie Doll's Julia). *Photo: Pat Fisher Pawlowicz.*

The larger breeds have the potential of excelling in Open competition in every discipline. Here, Lisa Leland-Courschenes and Welsh Cob Llanarth Trustful demonstrate the kind of dressage test that won them a USDF All Breeds award in 1993. *Photo: Bunny Ramsay.*

possibly more accepted or "suitable" population. This is simply a matter of niche, which is underscored by market demands. By taking one step sideways and reassessing the same breed's capabilities against the broader market realistically, however, you may find that what you've got are individuals superbly suited to the jumper ring, combined driving, combined training, or the hunt field—all places where athleticism, agility, "foot," and boldness are valued more than a daisy cutting stride attached to refined build. *This is not a reflection on the qualities of your breed.* It is simply a way of fitting a nice animal into the niche where it will have the opportunity to show off and live up to its innate potential, whatever that may be. This is the essence of the right pony for the right job.

The beauty of our major pony breeds is that they generally tend to be wonderful jacks of all trades. Most of them have the

Connemara Custusha's Cashel Rock (*Texas Hope x Springledge Taffy) and rider Connie Tuor outjumped bigger horses for many years and were instant crowd favorites wherever they went. *Photo: Connemara Country File.*

capability to do *well enough* in a number of different disciplines, and many breed societies offer extensive versatility awards programs that recognize this valuable trait. It's also unquestionably true that all ponies can be improved in their performances in a specific area by being given the benefit of correct and systematic schooling. Thus, if you're breeding a pony because you love the pony and feel that the niche is secondary, you can rest assured that with few exceptions your properly raised and prepared ponies will certainly be able to go out and hold their own under saddle, over fences, or in harness *up to a particular level and given the necessary foundation*. The upper limits of the pony's success in competition will then vary according to its build, individual talent, scope, and desire, as well as the access of its (equally talented and dedicated) rider to quality instruction, and plenty of exposure to mileage at shows or events.

Its eventual success at the *upper* levels of any discipline, however, may be dictated by the perceptions of an established marketplace, as well as by the judges who help to create and further these perceptions (sometimes unfortunate but generally true). Added to this are basic structural limitations of height, length of stride, or speed. The old saw that "a good big 'un will beat a good little 'un every time" has a certain degree of truth, in that the "little 'un" will be at a disadvantage in any situation in which size, stride, or sheer, raw power are deciding factors. This is not such an issue at the lower or even middle levels of most ridden competition, and may not be a hindering force at all in the driven disciplines. In both driving and in lower-level jumper classes, for instance, ponies frequently excel *because* their smaller stature and accompanying handiness allows them to cut corners and take risky lines that could leave a larger horse scrambling for its feet. Size becomes a greater factor in the ridden disciplines as distances and speeds grow tougher, fences higher and broader, and weight requirements heavier. And quality is often likely to be an issue in hunter classes where the refined elegance of a Thoroughbred is considered the standard.

Practical Research

If you're looking for ponies that can succeed consistently at the upper levels of a specific discipline, it helps to try to find out an approximate ratio of *how many* of that breed's registered individuals are already doing well there, instead of being swayed by the astonishing performance of one superstar that has benefited from a fortunate configuration of superb conformation, talent, topnotch training, superior riders, and a lot of exposure without regard to budget.

Say your aim is to raise really nice, solid combined training ponies suitable for a family to compete on safely and successfully for many years. Your favored breed has a couple of superstars at the upper levels that are very deservedly wowing all who see them and giving the breed a lot of great press. Are they flukes? Yes, probably. Few ponies from any breed will have the scope to succeed at the highest levels of most disciplines, and few owners of ponies have the skill, desire, or financial backing required to give themselves and their mounts the necessary time and training to attempt it. Added to this are the immense physical demands and staggering weight requirements made on a small frame during high-level competition, which makes no concessions to the size of the animal and adds yet more strain to backs and legs already pushed to the outer limits of their bearing capacity. Again, this is no slight to the pony. Event riders who have competed to the upper levels on pony breeds are quite open about saying that it was the combination of weight carried, speed required, and the sheer size and length of courses that finally limited the competitive lives of many of their smaller mounts, not any lack of heart, desire, or ability-per-size. These riders maintain that asking for efforts so testing and punishing of a game little animal becomes too unfair, when at a somewhat lower level the same ponies could compete happily for years as schoolmasters or the valued companions of riders with somewhat less ambitious goals than, say, Rolex Kentucky.

But let's put this in perspective. As a basis of comparison it can safely be said that few Thoroughbreds have what it takes to win a leg of the Triple Crown, either, and in fact it's estimated that only 7 percent of those that race will ever be stakes placed. Yet there are still an enormous number of Thoroughbreds out there that are useful racehorses.

So if you drop back to Training and Preliminary and find a dozen or so more of the above-mentioned superstars' brethren quietly doing a good job for their people, and if at Elementary and Novice you find another several dozen good campaigners with happy owners, impressed judges, fans who are looking for ponies "just like that one," and halfbreds from the same families that are doing equally well, then you're on to something. If further research through the breed's governing body shows you that the number of ponies you've seen in competition represents more than 10 percent of the total current registration, you're in business; you obviously like the right pony for the right reasons. To use the Thoroughbred racehorse comparison again, this is

All ponies were born to do double duty on the trail. Pictured here is Fjord BDF Toril (Solar x Zwantje). *Photo: Arthur Rivoire.*

greater than the number born each year that actually get to the races and win anything.

THE JUDGE'S POINT OF VIEW

The foregoing is your field research, easily undertaken by simple observation and familiarity with a certain breed and a certain discipline. Further study will show you how judges and professionals feel about the niche you've chosen for the ponies they see every week in competition in a variety of contexts. Most will agree that ponies are the mount of choice for children, from leadline straight through to the upper ranks of pony hunter competition or Pony Clubbing. Many more are very accustomed to seeing adults riding large ponies at all but the highest levels of combined training, and driving competitions consistently fill whole divisions designed for ponies handled by both amateur and professional adults. Some judges are becoming quite accepting of ponies as adult mounts in the burgeoning Adult Amateur divisions at numerous hunter and dressage shows, although this recognition is not without certain reservations.

The chief of these has to do with suitability, the measure of how well pony and rider are matched in terms of relative size, temperament, and ability, and what kind of picture they create in performance. In driving, it's obviously not an issue, and there are numerous outgrown children's ponies that reappear in second careers as a parent's favorite driving pony. In any ridden discipline that takes suitability of mount and rider into account, however, a 13.2-hand pony carrying a 180-pound adult will be marked down. It doesn't matter if the pony involved is thought by the owner to be well up to the weight. To a professional observing the two, the equation is unequal. The overall picture is of a rider overburdening a pony that would be much more suitable as a child's mount.

This isn't always mere prejudice. Judges and trainers base their opinions on an impressive number of years observing hundreds of ponies and riders matched both appropriately and oddly. The plain fact is that no matter how strongly built a pony may be mechanically, its back and legs will be under a great deal of strain when lugging a large adult around. Something six inches taller and equally strongly built would be able to distribute the same weight in balance far more efficiently, and therefore in theory should carry the rider for a longer period of time with less likelihood of injury or lameness developing. On the other hand, no small child is really going to have enough seat and leg to be in control of a very large horse if some freak occurrence spooks it. And a child would be hard pressed to groom, care for, tack up, or mount the animal without supervision. The pony is thus the ideal mount for the child.

This doesn't mean that adults shouldn't ride ponies that measure 13.2 hands; nor does it mean that children should not be on anything larger. A small adult may suit a broad, strong, athletic pony very nicely. A capable seven-year-old might be perfectly suitably mounted on a quiet large pony that's a bit on the narrow side. While a hot pony will never be considered suitable for a child, it may turn out to be a terrific and aggressive performer when ridden by an appropriately sized adult with the experience needed to channel its energy. A quiet, middle-aged packer, conversely, can be a wonderful choice for either a novice child or a timid adult whose initial aspirations go no farther than weekend hacks and the possible occasional local schooling show. As a breeder, one of your roles is to be aware of these diverse elements, and honest in any evaluation of the suitability of your ponies to the riders at which they're targeted.

An essential point for the breeder to remember is that *no* type of pony will be all things to all people, and that no amount of desire or dreaming will make it so. If your observation and experience show you that, in the eyes of the larger equine community, the kind of pony you're breeding simply will not be looked on favorably or will not have the conformation or ability to attain success at the levels of competition or in the discipline you most aspire to, you should listen. You may need to adjust your thinking on the niche you want to fill, and find a more practical set of goals. When the realities of what you have and what the marketplace demands come into alignment with your goals and desires, you'll be on the way to breeding the ponies of your dreams. Better yet, you'll be breeding ponies that can make the dreams of others come true.

Chapter

4

How to Read and Make
Use of a Pedigree

The study of pedigrees gives breeders a wonderful opportunity to become educated about the history and make-up of favored ponies. For those on tight budgets, the mixing and matching of pedigrees on paper is a safer method than experimenting with our dearly bought ponies. Pedigrees even hold the keys to certain bits of information that may prove vital to future matches that we hope will found a new dynasty of pony superiority. Do we wonder why the offspring of certain mares and stallions *always* excel in jumping? Comparing their pedigrees will tell us. Do we wonder why a certain even-tempered mare and stallion consistently produce hot and temperamental offspring? The pedigree holds the clues. Understanding the value of these clues can take a great deal of early guesswork out of a process that is at best always a calculated risk.

Many people find the very thought of pedigree study enough to send them straight to sleep. In recent years it's also become common to hear people say disparagingly that a pedigree is nothing but a list of names that is useless as a tool for comparison between individuals and families, or as an education in the creation of good sport horses or ponies. To raise sport horses, the reasoning goes, it's far more instructive to study genotype (the types of genes that are inherited by a pony or horse from each of its parents) and phenotype (a scientific way of saying "conformation," or the way a pony or horse looks as a result of the combination of inherited genes and the effects of the animal's environment) than to "waste time" on pedigrees. Others maintain that "you can't ride a pedigree," and point out the fact that superior sport horses come in an array of shapes, sizes, colors, and heritages that may sometimes leave us scratching our heads in bemusement.

Yet how many of these superior traits were deliberately selected for, and how many were the result of a lucky brush with the proven genetic power of hybrid vigor? How many of these individuals can be counted on to reproduce their greatest qualities consistently through further generations? And how on earth can a person make any realistic assessment of the probable inheritance of either a genotype or a phenotype without knowing which of the names in a pedigree are responsible for passing on which traits with any regularity?

To a rider, this may not matter. But a breeder's success is strictly related to an ability to produce superior athletes year after year. This requires more than a good eye and wonderful instincts. And while your success doesn't necessarily rest on your achieving an advanced degree in genetics, it will require a solid familiarity with the prominent families of your breed and how they react when intermixed with one another both within and without the confines of their specific groups.

Each name in the pedigree of a superior sport horse or pony is attended by a history of what it has accomplished, what its offspring and ancestors have accomplished, and even what its cousins, aunts, and uncles have accomplished, both in performance and as broodstock. There are dozens of volumes written on Thoroughbred pedigrees alone that are read and reread by serious breeders in a quest for the "nicks" (crossings of animals from certain families that seem to result in offspring of physical similarity and predictable ability, the stuff of every breeder's dreams), as well as the crosses and outcrosses that will allow them to raise better athletes and more winning competitors in all disciplines.

Our ponies deserve at least this much consideration. Knowing their parents and grandparents isn't nearly as telling as knowing their history to the fourth and even fifth generations, where all sorts of surprises (both pleasant and nasty) may reside. You need to know how lines nick, why they do well (or why they don't), who passes on what traits through the generations with the greatest predictability (or who doesn't), who is prepotent for the jumping ability you covet and why, whether your ponies are inbred and how closely, and what might happen to the future of your breeding program if you use Rock Handsome consistently on his nieces.

Anybody who has bred a few foals knows that a successful nick is produced by more than putting the season's winning pony stallion to their best mares. It isn't terribly uncommon to breed two apparently outstanding individuals and get something that you'd swear was a mistake. Looking at the two ponies involved on the basis of conformation, performance, and so on may not indicate why the mating didn't work as you'd wished. A study of the family tree, however, may turn up certain traits common to the bloodline(s) concerned that combined to strengthen the less attractive tendencies you'd hoped to eliminate.

THE NAME GAME

It's no wonder that many people find pedigree charts daunting or even completely incomprehensible. The first five generations of a pony's family tree contain sixty-two names—more than enough to make your eyes cross, if you're coming to the process with no prior experience. Most of us can't even trace our human families that far back. Fortunately, it's doubtful that you'll need to memorize this many generations for immediate purposes. The first three, which are genetically probably the most important when speaking of any real effect on inheritance, will be your most frequently looked-at reference. You'll find over time that the generations farther back will begin to make more sense as the names of the ponies they list cross your consciousness often enough to give you a reason to remember them.

The Four-Generation Pedigree—I

Pony's Name	Sire	Grandsire #1	Great-grandsire 1	Gr-Gr-Grandsire 1 Gr-Gr-Granddam 1
			Great-granddam 1	Gr-Gr-Grandsire 2 Gr-Gr-Granddam 2
		Granddam #1	Great-grandsire 2	Gr-Gr-Grandsire 3 Gr-Gr-Granddam 3
			Great-granddam 2	Gr-Gr-Grandsire 4 Gr-Gr-Granddam 4
	Dam	Grandsire #2	Great-grandsire 3	Gr-Gr-Grandsire 5 Gr-Gr-Granddam 5
			Great-granddam 3	Gr-Gr-Grandsire 6 Gr-Gr-Granddam 6
		Granddam #2	Great-grandsire 4	Gr-Gr-Grandsire 7 Gr-Gr-Granddam 7
			Great-granddam 4	Gr-Gr-Grandsire 8 Gr-Gr-Granddam 8

There are thirty ponies listed in the first four generations of any pedigree: Two in the second, eight in the third, and sixteen in the fourth. As you can see, the effect of one great-grandparent cannot be considered to be very large in this model.

Reading a pedigree is really quite simple. The first two lines after your pony's name and details of birth, size, etc., list its sire on the top line and its dam on the bottom. The second generation lists four grandparents, and the third lists eight great-grandparents, for a total of fourteen. The names of stallions always occupy the top, so that the male line progresses along the topline of the pedigree chart. The names of mares always occupy the bottom, and the female line is traced along the bottomline. Male and female families will thus always be referred to as *topline* or *tail male*, or *bottomline* or *tail female*.

Everybody in between is still there, too. If you hear references to a stallion's female family, you simply put your finger on the sire's dam and follow that line down his chart. For the dam's male family, follow her sire line up. No matter where on the pedigree you begin, the system is the same.

The Four-Generation Pedigree—II

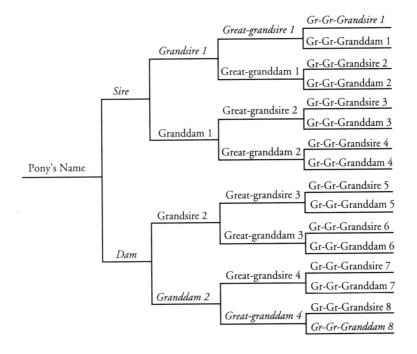

In this view, the tail male and tail female lines have been italicized for ease of reference. Male lines always go up and female lines always go down, no matter where you start on the pedigree. Clearly, thinking solely in terms of tail male or tail female lines forms a limited basis of comparison in that both ignore the presence of a great majority of other influential individuals. More information is needed to make it meaningful.

Meaning to Names

A pedigree that really is just a list of names largely unknown to you is *not* going to be a great deal of help in choosing stock unless you realize that each of these names stands for an individual that has history of either as a performer, a producer, or a relative of other ponies known to be successful in either (or both) of these categories. This calls for a *tabulated pedigree*, which lays out both the names of the ponies and short synopses of their records as performers, sires, or producers. It may also mention and use the records of close relatives that don't appear in the pedigree itself.

You can either tabulate a pedigree on your own or request it from your breed society. If your breed society doesn't offer this service, there are almost guaranteed to be members who think that stud books are great light reading, and who spend hours delving into the performance histories of all available members of the breed's various families. Ask around to find these wonderfully dedicated people, and make use of the research that they will gladly share with you. The hours they've spent ferreting out the quirks and surprises that exist in all equine bloodlines are most valuable, as are the complementary observations that range from opinionated to helpful to downright enlightening. All of this is an important addition to your body of knowledge, serving as a reference point that can be used at will while you learn about the ponies behind the names and their importance to their breed.

This is especially handy when, for instance, you're looking at a mare that never achieved anything of note in the showring for lack of opportunity or due to (nongenetically passed) lameness. A look at the successes of her dam's other foals (in particular) and those of her sire's other offspring (secondarily) can give you some inkling as to whether she's likely to carry the genes to produce the kind of athletes you're looking for. She may not, but her chances of success are certainly greater if she comes from a noted family of performers or producers than they are if her entire pedigree is full of ponies that have never achieved anything.

PEDIGREES AS A PREDICTION OF PHENOTYPE AND GENOTYPE

Each pony that appears in a pedigree contributes something to your pony's genetic makeup that will affect its conformation, soundness, athletic ability, and temperament. On the most simplistic of levels, you can judge roughly what kind of effect this will be by assigning values to the role of each name that appears—50 percent to sire and dam, 25 percent to grandparents, 12.5 percent to great-grandparents, and so forth. This is instantly complicated by the fact that you can't be exactly sure *which* 50 percent has been passed by each parent, or in what configuration. Obviously, all things being equal, a relationship based on one particular great-grandparent is not going to have an enormous effect on your final product. But this also depends on the heritability of certain traits, the prepotency (or genetic dominance) of certain animals in passing on specific important qualities or weaknesses, and the effects of linebreeding, inbreeding, and outcrossing. (See chapter 5 for more on these factors, and the appendix for further references to works that go into genetic study in the detail it deserves.)

If, for instance, the great-grandparent mentioned above had a dominant trait shared by other members of the family, or that combined with the same trait in another line (a condition in genetics that points to the presence of "homozygosity," in which alleles are always dominant and override other combinations), then chances are it will show up in your pony as well. This genetic hocus-pocus is the same thing that determined the many elements that combined to give you "your grandmother's eyes." On a basic level, it also describes how breeders begin *selecting* for specific positive traits to single out as breeding goals. Selecting (or deliberately breeding for) certain dominant tendencies is the basis of the formation of every breed, and eventually determines not only its shape and size, but its color, substance, and ability to run, jump, or pull.

Selection for certain specific tendencies can backfire, however. Occasionally certain recessive weaknesses, or those that have not been visible because they've been "disguised" by visible dominant traits, can "ride in" on the coattails of dominant genes, and make an unwelcome appearance when combined with the same recessive allele in another pony. This explains the seemingly incomprehensible mistakes that occur in every breeder's life, most of which aren't really as mysterious as they seem when studied more closely.

Once you recognize the names in any pedigree and can recall what it is about them that either rings warning bells or elicits a positive image, patterns of similarity will begin to emerge that illustrate corresponding tendencies in conformation, temperament, and athleticism—for good *and* ill. You may find that certain ponies that consistently appeal to you for any number of reasons are in fact prepotent for some combination of desirable traits that are common to the whole family. These families do exist in every breed. You may find yourself discussing the ins and outs of the fact that that the offspring of stallion X always produce incredible jumpers when bred to the mares of family Y, whereas the mares of family Y produce nothing but lunatics if bred to the offspring of stallion Z. *Genetically* speaking, there is a host of reasons for why this is the case. *Practically* speaking, your knowledge of pedigrees and your experience in seeing genetic effects on the hoof can serve as a code that is extremely valuable when selecting both broodstock and the matings designed to produce your next generation of good ponies. The ability to translate print into performance removes at least a few of the surprises that may lie in wait further down the road.

From "List of Names" to Tabulated Pedigree

Tabulated pedigrees give valuable information on size, color, performance, and the ability of each family member to pass on its best characteristics—all vital to breeders interested in a specific line of ponies. In addition to this information, a tabulated pedigree usually carries registration numbers, which have not been added in this example.

Turkdean Sword Dance has been a Supreme Champion in hand and in harness.

Sire: Turkdean Cerdin: Champion Mountain and Moorland Ponies of Britain Show 1967. Supreme in Hand and Reserve Overall Supreme Champion P.O.B.

			Llanarth Cerdin
Turkdean Sword Dance Pal., 13.3, 1968	Turkdean Cerdin Pal., 13.2, 1965	Llanarth Firel – Pal., 14.0, 1962	Llanarth Cerdin
			Llanarth Firelight
		Revel Romance – Ch., 12.0, 1954	Criban Winston
			Revel Ruby
	Llanarth Dancing Satellite – Ch., 13.0, 1958	Fronarth What Ho – Gr., 12.0, 1951	Dinarth What Ho
			Fron Arth Queen Bee
		Llanarth Flying Saucer – Ch. Rn., 13.2, 1951	Llanarth Braint
			Llanarth Rocket

1968. Ridden Champion, P.O.B. and National Pony Society Summer Shows 1972. Sire of Chalkhill Dragonfly (Supreme Champion in hand and ridden), Wyedean Carys (Youngstock Champion), etc.

Dam: Llanarth Dancing Satellite: Dam and grand-dam of Champion Section C and Section D Cobs.

Paternal 2nd Sire: Llanarth Firel: Champion in hand and in harness. Winner WPCS Performance Awards 1972. Gelded 1965.

Paternal 2nd Dam: Revel Romance: Prize winner. Dam of: Turkdean Cerdin (see above), Turkdean Gaffer (English Section C Premium 1972), Turkdean Idris (English Section C Premium 1983), etc.

Maternal 2nd Sire: Fronarth What Ho: Many times Royal Welsh Show Champion harness pony.

Maternal 2nd Dam: Llanarth Flying Saucer: Royal Welsh Overall Section C Champion 1965. Dam of: Llanarth Dancing Satellite (see above), Llanarth Flying Comet (Royal Welsh Show Champion 1974, 1976, 1977 and 1978; Twice Lloyd's Bank Champion), Llanarth Sian (P.O.B. M&M Champion), etc.

Chapter

5

THE INBRED, THE LINEBRED, AND THE OUTCROSSED

Inbreeding, linebreeding, and outcrossing are all terms describing the various systems for mixing ponies' bloodlines to achieve a certain consistency of genotype and phenotype. Used wisely, they provide educated breeders with an assortment of valuable tools to help determine the direction, scope, and control of a well-planned breeding program. Each plays an important role, both in meeting the individual needs of a small farm, and, in the larger context, of the preservation and maintenance of a breed and its chief qualities. Defined briefly:

Inbreeding is the mating of ponies that are extremely closely related to one another—full sister to full brother, sire (or dam) to daughter (or son), and in some cases the matings of half siblings, or of aunts and uncles with nephews or nieces. Because it concentrates genes for weaknesses as well as those for strengths, inbreeding can be either wildly successful or a terrible failure. Its use thus demands an ability to ride with the failures and a willingness to cull frequently and heartlessly to make sure that those failures aren't repeated.

Linebreeding is a more conservative form of inbreeding. It usually involves the crossing of more distant relatives in the

interest of concentrating the genetic effects of a certain stallion
or mare, and increasing the chances of developing stock prepotent for some of that individual's superior traits. The more often
this mare or stallion's name appears, and the closer to the front
of the pedigree it is, the more intense the linebreeding has
become.

Inbreeding or Linebreeding

The pedigree below illustrates a common form of
inbreeding, in which two half-siblings are mated in an
attempt to strengthen the effects of a common ancestor
(bold type) by intensifying the presence of her desirable
genetic material.

Round Robin's Mountain Echo	An Tostal	*Tooreen Laddie	Inchagoill Laddie
			Grey Swan
		*Clare Dun	**Lavalley Rebel**
			Miss McGauley
	Wicklow Mtn. Rose Bay	MacDara	Dun Lorenzo
			Dolan Rose
		*Clare Dun	**Lavalley Rebel**
			Miss McGauley

In the second example, the pony has been *linebred* to a
common ancestor (bold type) in a less condensed and

thus theoretically less risky fashion that still has the potential to intensify specific desirable traits of a common ancestor.

Tre Awain De Valera	Tre Awain Roderick O'Conor	MacDara	Dun Lorenzo
			Dolan Rose
		*Lonely Cottage	Carna Dun
			Ballinahinch Daughter
	*Clonkeehan Lent Lily	Clonkeehan Nimbus	Camlin Cicada
			Dark Winter
		*Clonkeehan Tiger Lily	MacDara
			*Clonkeehan Easter Lily

An *outcrossed* pedigree will contain no repeated names, and thus should contain a greater *diversity* of genetic material to be passed on to further generations.

Some authorities argue that linebreeding and inbreeding are the same thing, and in fact the delineation can become a bit muddy. To some people, for instance, the idea of mating half siblings—even when their unrelated halves bear nothing in common—is inbreeding as surely as the crossing of full siblings would be. This sentiment also holds true in the example of breeding uncle to niece or nephew to aunt. To others, these options might be considered a completely acceptable form of selecting for specific traits that will "stamp" a certain line of ponies in a desired way.

For the average breeder, a more conservative course of line-breeding will probably be safer and ultimately of more value to the health and success of a herd than a more closely related bunch. How do you tell the difference for practical purposes? Well, if your pony's pedigree has the same name appearing twice in the first three or four generations—preferably a couple of generations back and surrounded by nonrelations—it's not too closely bred. But if that name appears more often, or if the fourth generation contains essentially only one stallion or mare name, your pony can pretty safely be called inbred.

Outcrossing, as you might expect given the above, is the mating of animals that are not related to one another. It's also a term used for breeding away from certain families and bloodlines that have become too concentrated and need an infusion of "outside blood" to regain the greater degree of health, fertility, and ability that might have been lost through the inbreeding process.

Of these three, the subject of inbreeding has generated heated debate among pony breeders for many years, and with good reason: Used indiscriminately it can destroy a breed within a very few generations. Yet inbreeding is also the way in which breed type becomes established in the first place, be it naturally selected or "manmade." We tend to think of feral groups of horses and ponies as being more naturally outcrossed than domestic stock due to wide geographical movement and the shifting supremacy of older and younger stallions. In fact, these groups' gene pools are fairly restricted. There are only so many miles that a horse or pony will cover in its lifetime, even in a natural state. Most groups of animals tend to stay within certain geographical boundaries unless some powerful outside influence (whether human or environmental) steps in to change a habitual pattern of movement and behavior. In that the genes of the most hardy and long-lived animals will be passed on most frequently, prepotency for whatever traits allow their offspring to thrive in a particular set of conditions will be set early on, and breed type established. Were it not for a certain amount of inbreeding, we wouldn't have breeds recognizable as separate entities, or that are suited to a wide variety of different geographical, climatic, and athletic pursuits. Nor would our "purebred" ponies be capable of breeding true to their type.

But given the fact that all horses and ponies are inbred to begin with (the less numerous breeds to a greater degree than the more numerous), further tampering with something that in effect narrows the gene pool even more drastically can be dangerous to the health of a breed. This is especially true when it is used indiscriminately or in ignorance of the possible ramifications of mating two superior but very closely related animals. As discussed earlier, it's far better to be aware of the relationships between your stallion and mares on paper right from the start than to realize several disasters later that Old Mad Molly, universally renowned for her savagery and lameness, appears five times in the first four generations of the beautiful but useless ponies you've bred with such hope. Education is definitely in order.

GENETICS AT ITS MOST BASIC

On the simplest possible level, *genes* are pieces of DNA molecules that cause certain proteins to be created within a cell and dictate every heritable trait (i.e., one that can be passed on rather than one that is dictated by environmental factors) that makes a pony. Genetic information is carried in the cell nucleus by *chromosomes*. Various configurations of genes control everything from color to white markings to speed to substance to temperament. Genes carry pairs of *alleles* that modify their given traits to a lesser or greater extent. When paired, these alleles are said to be *dominant* if the traits they express override other traits found on their corresponding allele. They are said to be *recessive* if these traits are unexpressed due to the presence of some other overriding dominant allele.

A gene is said to be *homozygous* if the paired alleles are both dominant, in which case that pony will *always* pass on a dominant allele to its offspring, and the offspring will *always* show that dominant trait. It is said to be *heterozygous* if its paired alleles contain one dominant and one recessive element. In this case, the dominant allele will be the one that is physically expressed, but the recessive allele is still present, and could be passed on to the pony's offspring.

To use an example of how this works, let's look at the color grey. All ponies that are not grey carry two alleles for nongrey coloring, which is shown as "gg," a recessive configuration that will always be overridden by other colors. But grey itself is a dominant color, and will override all other colors if even one "G" allele appears. Therefore, your grey pony will carry alleles that combine to make either "Gg" (one dominant/one recessive, or heterozygous) or "GG" (two dominant, or homozygous).

Inheritance of Grey Coloring

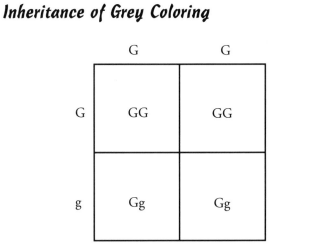

Each Parent carries two alleles for the grey (G) or nongrey (g) color. Each will pass one of these on to its offspring. Both parents in this example will look grey because grey (G) is always dominant over nongrey (g). In this example, all offspring will receive one dominant G allele and thus appear grey. Those which receive two dominant genes (GG) will be homozygous (i.e., capable of passing on only a grey allele), and all of their subsequent offspring will be grey, no matter what they are bred to. However, the offspring that receive one nongrey (Gg) gene will be heterozygous, and will produce some nongreys, as below:

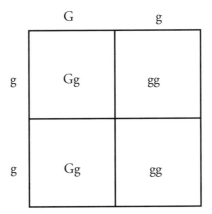

Here, 50 percent of the offspring will be grey, and 50 percent nongrey.

Say you want to get another grey pony by breeding yours, so you breed to a lovely grey stallion, and are crushed when you get a bay foal. What happened? The most obvious answer is that both ponies were *heterozygous* greys (Gg), which passed on only their "g" (recessive, or nongrey) alleles to combine. The result: a nongrey pony. If either pony had passed on the "G" instead, it would have combined with your mare's "g" to make another heterozygous grey. If, however, your pony or the stallion you bred her to was a *homozygous* ("GG") grey, you would have gotten a grey foal no matter what. The allele "G" is always dominant.

The subject of color dominance can be further illustrated by the case of Norwegian Fjords, which are *always* some permutation of dun. All other possible color genes were selected out of the breed so long ago that they no longer exist in the fullbred pony.

The situation with genes and alleles isn't always this cut-and-dried, but the basics remain pretty much the same. Each parent of a pony passes on 50 percent of its genetic material to each one of its offspring, a further 25 percent of which material was received from each of *its* parents in turn. Say you're mating two ponies that are of the same breed but have nothing in their pedigrees in common. Depending on how the 50 percent of genetic material is configured, all of the offspring of this particular pairing could conceivably look quite different. If this is the case, the good news is that no major bad traits are turning up, as these are frequently recessive and are thus unexpressed unless concentrated in a way that makes them homozygous. Therefore, your ponies should be relatively free of congenital disease or lameness, and should achieve the *average* height, speed, ability, and fertility of their breed. The bad news is that the lack of dominance for certain traits that you think are important (whether jumping ability, temperament, bone, or something else) may be keeping you from getting the consistently good quality ponies you really want. This is a classic outcrossing dilemma—safe, but not necessarily spectacular.

SELECTING FOR A DESIRED TRAIT

Here's how the theory might work in practice. Say your mare has a grandsire that you particularly admired because of a certain set of traits that he passed on to many of his offspring with great consistency (we'll use a stallion for this illustration, but it could just as easily be a mare). Maybe he was unusually correct through the limbs, or had a lovely freedom of movement, or a remarkable temperament, or incredible jumping ability. Maybe he had a combination of these things. His granddaughter, if you've been lucky in your choice of mares, might have inherited some of these qualities from him, but she wouldn't have gotten more than 25 percent of his genetic material, and that will have been altered in some way by the presence of the other 75 percent of the genes that she's inherited from other ancestors. If you breed her to totally unrelated ponies, the effects of that superlative grandsire will become even further diluted, until the qualities you wanted from that individual become all but negligible.

To make sure that the inheritance of that lovely pony will be passed on with greater consistency, you may very well choose to breed to another son or a grandson of his that expresses his strengths to a large degree. You could even go so far as to flirt with inbreeding, and breed your mare back to her grandsire or an equally lovely full brother of his. *The point of the operation is that the resulting offspring will have a greater concentration of the desired pony's genetic material, and thus a greater likelihood of showing the same qualities.* This concentration of genetic material also results in a higher incidence of homozygosity for certain heritable traits, and thus may actually become dominant for them. If this occurs, the stallion or mare that results from the mating may be *prepotent* for those desirable traits, which means that he or she will tend to pass them on to subsequent offspring with a great deal of consistency due to the dominance (or homozygosity) of the alleles concerned. If you hear breeders talk about a pony that "stamps his get" (or "her produce"), this is what they mean. The classic example of this is Justin Morgan, who stamped an entire breed more or less single-handedly. Current thinking dictates that the original Justin Morgan must himself have been extremely "closebred" or inbred to have been so prepotent for his qualities. The further crossing of his offspring with their half siblings and other close relatives served to develop a breed of horse that was absolutely distinct in type within a very few generations.

So, you may well be wondering, if linebreeding and inbreeding have the effect of creating superior athletes through concentrating all that great genetic stuff, why aren't we doing it all the time? Well, for several reasons. The main one is that when certain genetic information is being combined in a highly concentrated way, it also strengthens whatever weaknesses have been masked by dominant genes in an outcrossed environment. Let's say, for example, that although Granddaddy Stallion was full of absolutely marvelous qualities that made your palms itch with desire, he also had very bad feet. Perhaps bad feet are

Inheritance of Bad Feet

Using whatever combination of genes that determine bad feet as an example of an undesirable trait, let's say that you have a mare who is otherwise superb, but has feet that are less than desirable, considering breed standards (ff). To improve the situation, you breed her to a stallion whose feet are wonderful and who always sires ponies with good feet (FF), as in (A) below.

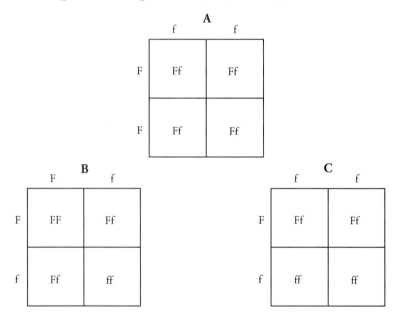

All the resulting offspring in this model will have good feet, but will carry one allele for bad feet (masked by the dominant F, which in our very over simplified example stands for good feet). If one is bred to another Ff pony, there will be a 25 percent chance of getting offspring with bad feet (B). If *that* pony is bred to an Ff pony, the potential for bad feet grows to 50 percent (C). Clearly, selection work can work to your disadvantage as well as your advantage, unless you continually use breeding stock prepotent for desirable characteristics.

almost unknown in your breed, so this aberration went all but unnoticed as long as the stallion in question was bred to mares whose feet were as good as the breed average. The bad feet in this case remain recessive, masked by the breed's dominant genetic inclination to good feet.

But when you start dabbling in linebreeding and inbreeding, whatever genetic combination occurred to give that pony bad feet will be made stronger by the concentration of that trait. It's thus possible that when you breed your mare to a related stallion (both with decent feet—you may not even be aware of the "bad feet problem" that existed in Grandpa), you may be shocked to be presented with a foal that typifies everything you wished for, except for having terrible feet. A large breeder with time and money to spare may look at this situation as a learning experience, cull the foal from the breeding herd, and breed the mare back in hopes of getting a foal with better feet. If the second attempt succeeds, that foal may stay in the herd to carry on. The unexpressed tendency to bad feet will remain recessive unless a further association with another pony with the same genetic concentration brings it out again.

But a small breeder may not have the luxury of trying that cross repeatedly and culling the less-than-perfect result, and may choose to keep the foal as a breeding prospect despite its feet. In this case, the genetic code for bad feet will be passed on yet again, perhaps now as a dominant trait. And so the erstwhile breeder has unwittingly loosed a heritable defect into the gene pool of a breed that heretofore had not been known for bad feet except in rare cases.

CULLING AS QUALITY CONTROL

To prevent this from happening, all situations in which linebreeding and inbreeding are used extensively require rigorous culling of stock that doesn't live up to a hoped-for standard. The goal you're seeking to achieve here is prepotence for superior qualities and the elimination of weaknesses. In a natural system, a similar type of mating pattern might occur, with close relatives mating and producing offspring that we would consider to be very inbred. The difference in such a system of natural selection is that we never see the mistakes—the job of selection is undertaken harshly and objectively by the environment in which the ponies live. If they inherit qualities that enhance their longevity and ability to thrive in a certain set of conditions, they live. If they inherit weaknesses (like the above-mentioned bad feet) that keep them from thriving, they die. It's for this simple reason that so many of our pony breeds are renowned for their hardiness, soundness, and brains.

Natural selection is thus as much a factor of the intertwined forces of inheritance and environment as is the artificial selection of human beings trying to control both elements to develop strains of ponies with the ability to thrive in a less natural but equally specific setting. We aren't likely to put a pony down just because it turns out to be a weed or to have crooked legs, especially if we can find a loving home for it. But we should have the sense to realize that a pony with congenital defects of any kind must not be considered a useful breeding prospect. No matter how good the blood behind it is, its chances of passing on its heritable faults are far too great to make the risk worthwhile, especially if there are similarly bred ponies available that can meet the breed's standard better.

THE SHRINKING GENE POOL

The other drawback of consistent linebreeding or inbreeding is that over time, if you continue to breed close relatives through a number of generations, it decreases the gene pool to the extent that many good qualities will be lost in the shuffle. By definition, inbreeding reduces the numbers of gene pairs that can be inherited by any offspring, which is why inbred ponies are so prepotent for certain traits. The process of inbreeding has simply eliminated a wide variety of alleles from the genetic material of those ponies. It's thus quite true that inbred systems over time will suffer from a general loss of size, fertility, and vigor. These things are improved by *heterosity*, or the presence of a large variety of genes. The more inbred the pony, the more homozygous its genotype, and the less access it has to traits that are dependent on a variety of alleles for their expression.

This loss of vigor, and the attendant genetic weaknesses that occur with it, are not *created* by inbreeding *in and of itself*. These can be traits that may have existed in a recessive state and have been exposed due to the consistency of their concentration by breeding back into the lines of ponies that carry them. Or it may just as easily be that traits that include vigor, fertility, and freedom from genetic weaknesses rely on heterosity to be expressed and maintained in a healthy state.

FINDING THE RIGHT BALANCE

Linebreeding and inbreeding should always go hand in hand with judicious outcrossing to ensure the continued health, vigor, and athletic performance of your ponies. Linebreeding will produce the wonderful individuals that you dreamed of, but it has been proven over and over again that the greatest "nicks" (matings that consistently produce outstanding performers) are often those that occur between two unrelated (though possibly linebred within themselves) individuals whose genes combine to produce what's known as *hybrid vigor*.

As mentioned in Chapter 4, geneticists admit that they aren't quite sure why it is that hybrid vigor works, but there is no arguing with the fact that in certain circumstances the mating of two unrelated lines (or two unrelated breeds) results in the creation of ponies that are far superior to their parents. This is especially true in the context of traits that are controlled by a number of different genes, rather than those that are expressed very specifically. Examples of the latter would include things such as jumping ability (which, with speed, has proven itself to be highly heritable) and intelligence. The former consists of the variety of alleles controlling traits such as color and temperament. Size, which is genetically programmed, can be affected strongly by environmental stimuli such as starvation, being a twin, etc. Bone (the circumference of the cannon below the knee) is considered to be moderately heritable, and along with substance seems to rely in part on its genetic dominance (or lack of same) in certain breeds or families. Thus it is that increased heterosity—the exposure through breeding to a broader array of genetic material—increases the chances of a given pony inheriting the combination of material that will result in sporting animals of superior ability in many disciplines.

The "Nicked" Pedigree

The pedigree below illustrates an early foundation in U.S. Connemaras famed for producing superior athletes. At one time, this was thought to have a lot to do with the genetic influence of the Thoroughbred Little Heaven, who was used briefly for new blood.

(Sons and Daughters of)	*Tooreen Laddie	Inchagoill Laddie	Rebel
			Dooyer Lass
		Grey Swan	Unknown C.P.
			Unknown C.P.
	*ErinBay	Little Heaven (TB)	Bala Hissar
			Outport
		Glen Nelly	Gil
			Nelly Carroll

A student of pedigrees would say rather that the offspring's consistent quality was due to a genetic "nick" formed by *Tooreen Laddie and Glen Nelly (in bold), as illustrated by comparing both the above pedigree and the Irish one below:

			Inchagoill Laddie
Tulira Mairtin	Tooreen Ross	*Tooreen Laddie	
			Grey Swan
		Wayfarer	Unknown C.P.
			Unknown C.P.
	Glen Nelly	Gil	Inchagoill Laddie
			Golden Gleam
		Nelly Carroll	Unknown C.P.
			Unknown C.P.

This pony's offspring formed a similar dynasty in Ireland and England of ponies with exceptional jumping ability and competitive talent. Note also the linebreeding to Inchagoill Laddie (in bold). Of such bits and pieces of information are pedigree addicts made!

SEARCHING FOR THE MAGIC NICK

If the genetic material handed on by each of your ponies has an affinity for that of its mate (or more correctly, if the alleles concerned combine in a way that produces dominance in certain important respects while masking any recessive traits that would be undesirable), then you've got the pony of your dreams—not just once, but repeatedly. The discovery of these nicks is, of course, 75 percent legwork, 20 percent intuition, and 5 percent sheer dumb luck. Even geneticists admit freely that luck, chance, and serendipity play a great part in the final genetic inheritance of full brothers and sisters. For this reason you're likely in a single family of ponies to get one superstar, a couple of above average to decent performers, a washout, a sire and producer worth their weight in gold, and one or two that are strictly average.

The superponies may not even pass their abilities on to the next generation with anywhere near the consistency of their parents. The variety of combined attributes that has made them great can combine with the next generation's breedings in ways that are varied and erratic, depending on the genetic material added by the selected mare or stallion bred to. And so the cycle begins again—of whether to linebreed and how much, of whether to inbreed and to whom, and of when to outcross and which lines will provide the needed "zing" to create a new generation of superstars. Again, it's your knowledge that will increase your chances of succeeding.

Chapter

6

THE PERFECT BROODMARE

M ost breeders agree that the real cornerstone of their opera-
tions is a good broodmare, and that the right mare will be
the single purchase that, over time, will dictate the success or
failure of your breeding program. Why is this? A mare can produce only twelve or at the most maybe fifteen offspring in a busy
lifetime, as opposed to a stallion's ability to sire three or four
times that in a year, and her influence on a breed is quieter and
takes longer to evaluate than that of a stallion. It's also true that
she may never achieve the glory or publicity of a stallion that can
stand at stud while simultaneously carrying on with a brilliant
performance career.

Yet out of all the nice ponies that will come and go throughout your life as a breeder and owner, your foundation mare will
be the one that keeps reproducing herself year after year, the one
that gives you your winners, your best advertising, your most
consistent product, your line's own particular "look," and new
generations of good hunters, driving ponies, or producers like
herself. Genetics aside, most breeders are in agreement that on a
practical level the mare is responsible for 60 percent (some say
75 percent!) of the resulting foals' quality, mind, attitude, and
ability. Whole dynasties can be and have been built around the
progeny and descendants of a single mare. That's why she's quite
literally called a foundation mare, and why you'll sometimes find

the photo of a dowdy, swaybacked old girl who lost her figure about ten foals ago tucked into the middle of an otherwise glossy farm brochure. She's the one who built the farm and kept it afloat through even the driest years.

There's rarely a price big enough to buy this great brood-mare from the fortunate person who found her as a two-year-old and has maintained her for twenty years with growing respect and homage. The discovery of one or several fillies that will establish your farm's breeding program as a predictable and successful entity thus becomes your first practical priority.

Simple logic dictates that this shouldn't be all that diffi-cult—you simply find a mare that epitomizes all the best attributes of her breed or class, buy her, and the rest will be his-tory. Nature is rarely that straightforward, however, and the pony business is littered with failed breeders who believed erron-eously that a successful program could be built by buying up the top winners of this year's youngstock classes and mating them with the most popular stallions of the moment. In reality, the prettiest mares are not necessarily the best producers, and some exceptionally lovely mares never produce a foal as nice as them-selves. Other plain little things produce consistently better than themselves. And the full sister of a leading broodmare may not necessarily produce offspring of equal quality.

Some mares have wonderful foals no matter which stallion they're bred to; others do well only when nicked with a very spe-cific individual or family. Some mares are written off early as bad producers simply because they've never been bred to the right stallion *for them*. Others are simply not great, ever. This doesn't mean that they're unworthy mares that lack quality, breeding, or athletic ability. Just as all colts born are not destined to be stal-lion quality, not all fillies are going to be broodmare material, and only about the best 50 percent of all mares deserve to be bred. While it's always worthwhile to breed good performance mares a couple of times to see if they pass on their talent, it isn't a disaster if they don't. In the long run, these mares, like the thou-sands of geldings that give their owners years of pleasure and competitive success, will do you far more good as outstanding competitors than they will as second-rate producers.

Although it may be tempting to use a mare like this nontypical Connemara in a breeding program simply because of her quality, it could be a real mistake unless you know for certain that her off-spring will be true to type—a gamble at best. Mares like this are frequently better off in performance or in crossbreeding programs, where their refinement can be an asset. *Photo: Stan Phaneuf.*

Breed type is essential in choosing an ideal foundation mare. The better choice for breeding is this Connemara, Bantry Bay's Caitlin (Spring Ledge Bantry Bay x Lynfields Trudy). *Photo: Stan Phaneuf.*

THE "FIRST-GLANCE PHENOMENON"

Finding the perfect mare obviously begins with superior conformation and breed type. But even before that, there's the
importance of what could be called the "first-glance phenomenon," which is a matter of instinct or intuition. The first-glance
phenomenon states that if you aren't immediately attracted to the
mare or filly that you're looking at, you probably shouldn't buy
her. Even if she's drop-dead gorgeous and just won on the line at
Devon, you may never really like her if you weren't instantly
struck by her in the field or barn or showring. You may find, in
fact, that as you watch endless mares and fillies parade in a well-
filled class, your eye keeps returning to one that nobody else
seems to have noticed much. You try not to look at her, but you
keep going back. Maybe there's a sweetness and honesty about
her, or a workmanlike attitude, or even a glint of humor and
intelligence that's attractive. Maybe it's a particularly light way of
going or a lovely depth and breadth. Pay attention to this instinct,
because whatever draws you is likely a quality that is really
important to your feelings of how a pony mare should be made.
She deserves a second look no matter where she ends up in that
day's placings.

It's during this second look that you have to put away your
emotion, and take a mental razor to her conformation.

ASSESSING THE POTENTIAL BROODMARE

Each prospective breeder will have a slightly different agenda
when describing the perfect broodmare. But generally speaking,
a good broodmare prospect *must* demonstrate the qualities that
are essential to your breed's standard, and be sound, sane, and
free from genetic weaknesses. The commonly heard refrain that
"She's too lame (or crazy or allergic to dust) to show, so we'll just
breed her" is a terrible recipe for raising successful sport horses.
It's even worse when speaking of ponies, which are universally
valued for their health, soundness, sense, and freedom from
genetic defects.

For breed type and quality, it would be hard to improve on the exceptional Welsh Cob mare Fair Tegolin of Penrhyn (Dafydd Y Brenin Cymraeg x Nebo Fair Lady). While she is the image of many of the best attributes of her own breed, she also typifies the strong, ruggedly beautiful traits common to all native ponies.

Your examination will start at the bottom, by looking at feet that are hard, round, of evenly matched size, and neither too low (which leads to bruising) or too high (which can indicate a tendency to a clubfoot) in the heel. Heels should also be open, not contracted. The color of feet is thought to be very important by some people, of little importance to others. In general, however, a white or striped foot (quite common in grey ponies or those with white stockings) is not a fault, and the old saw that insists that a white foot is softer than a dark one has been largely discredited. Remember, however, that most ponies ought to be capable of doing light work throughout their lives unshod, and many are capable of years of work with only front shoes. The main point is that *good feet are essential*. This is not a place to cut corners.

It's pretty uncommon to find long, sloping pasterns like those found in Thoroughbreds in any pony, but this is not critical as long as they are of sufficient length (not giving the appearance of being nonexistent) and slope (matching the slope of the foot, but not straight up and down). The very upright pastern may suggest a tendency to navicular disease from the extra pounding or jarring that the front feet will take as a result, although on the whole, pony breeds don't tend to be prone to this condition. Too long and weak a pastern, with too much flex and an accompanying foot that is low or underslung in the heel, can lead to bruising of the foot or injury to the soft tissue surrounding the fetlock during the stress of heavy work over fences or across country.

Legs must be straight, all pointing in the same direction, with dense, flat bone, broad forearms and gaskins, and short cannons. Long, slender cannons are not as strong. Legs that deviate from plumbline straight when looked at from the front or side should be avoided, if at all possible. Crooked legs are highly heritable, and lead to deviations in movement that indicate potential unsoundness.

Other pass-bys are ponies that are over or back at the knee, tied in below the knee, or that have small or round knee, hock, and fetlock joints. A leg that isn't strongly enough built, or that isn't lined up properly, puts immense strain on the joints, the feet, and all of the limb's supportive tendons and ligaments. Add the stress of basic conformational imbalance to the heavy load of a rider and the punishment of strenuous activities, and you usually end up with a pony that can't last in a competitive environment for very long before going lame. Natural selection has favored ponies whose legs are strong and well built, so that it's more common to find good limbs and feet than bad ones. Deviations and weaknesses must thus be considered grave faults in a pony destined to be a broodmare.

Some length of back is normal in a pony broodmare. After all, you want her to have plenty of room to carry a foal, especially if you intend to use her as a cross with larger pony or smaller Thoroughbred stallions. A long back that is accompanied by a lack of depth through the heartgirth, a poorly sprung ribcage,

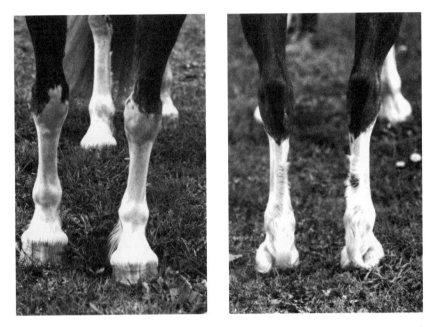

Large, flat joints; short cannons with an abundance of dense, flat bone; and hard feet are critical. Ponies do not necessarily have the ultralong, sloping pasterns we associate with some horse breeds. As long as the slope is adequate, the pastern/hoof angle correct, and the feet of good size and shape, this shouldn't lead to any unsoundness problems. This mare's slight cowhocks should not be a great concern if the rest is good enough.

and a tendency to be "herring gutted" will be weak, and should be avoided. But moderate length with a matching depth and breadth through the body that flows into a broad, well-muscled loin, croup, and hindquarter is perfectly acceptable.

We all think of ponies, or small ponies, anyway, as being as broad as they are tall. This can be the case, but it can go to extremes, especially if you're breeding ponies for children. An overly broad chest and barrel can hamper a pony's ability to move freely as well as being problematical for short-legged riders. Narrowness is not a good thing in a breeding prospect, however. Ponies should appear foursquare and solid, and you definitely don't want a mare that gives the impression of both forelegs coming out of the same slot.

Whether the croup and hindquarters are broad and level or broad and sloping is a matter of breed identification, but the emphasis is on "broad," when looked at from above and behind.

Ponies sometimes have a tendency to be undefined in the withers (some don't appear to have them at all), and this, combined with a short, thick neck, can combine to give a heavy or "hammy" look about the shoulder. Try to find a mare that is at least clean around the wither area, with a neck that meets the wither and shoulder smoothly. People put a great deal of stress on the idea of a sloping shoulder as a measure of good movement, but the angle of the shoulder is actually only a part of the equation. Having assessed that, now look at the angle from the point of the shoulder to the point of the elbow. Does it match the angle of the shoulder? Is it flat (approaching the horizontal) or acute? The more acute angle points to a *freer* shoulder with legs that swing forward more efficiently and offer a longer stride. *This does not mean that the pony will be a daisy cutter.* Most native breeds aren't, and most judges of them prefer them not to be, feeling that the long, low-moving pony is one that won't do well in trappy country or over fences. If you're breeding only for dressage, this may not be an issue. But it will behoove you to learn how to see movement that is free and loose, even if it is a little on the round side. The efficient mover will always have more scope, and if your intent is to breed for an Adult Amateur or highly competitive Junior market, this is vital.

The mare should move straight. When you see her from the side, she should move freely without interfering. When viewed from the front and back, her forefeet should move in a straight line along their track, without paddling (feet twisting outward) or winging (feet twisting inward). If you have to make a choice between two evils, paddling is the lesser one, since it rarely leads to a pony hitting itself. Remember that what you're choosing is a broodmare first, a performer second. If your mare doesn't move straight, at least a percentage of her offspring won't either. Why pass on faults if you have a choice not to?

Active hocks are essential. It's easy to be fooled into thinking that a pony with extravagant foreleg action is a good mover.

Given that ponies are natural athletes, strong hindquarters are essential.

A beautiful head and expressive eye.

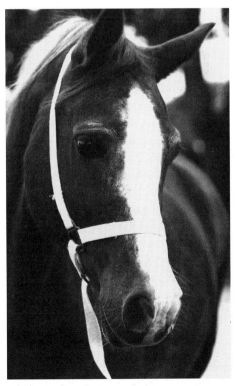

But before going into too many raptures over such a mare, take a good look at whether the hindlegs are equally energetic. Remember that the rear end is what drives forward movement (not to mention jumping ability), and this requires active hocks that reach well under the pony when she moves. A slight tendency to cowhocks might be okay, but movement that is anything other that straight and true is a major fault. There are plenty of ways for a pony to hurt itself when competing in any athletic endeavor without its basic conformation being its greatest liability, and a pony that doesn't move well behind will be weaker in heavy training, more prone to injury, and more likely to step on itself.

Ideas about what constitute a desirable head, neck, and topline can be pretty subjective from one breeder (and one breed) to another. We all fall for pretty heads, but they aren't the element on which our breeding programs' success will hang, and you certainly can't ride one. You do have to look at it every day, however. In general, if it supports the breed standard, has a big, kind, expressive eye (which, by the way, can make a plain head look prettier), and doesn't offend you in any way, it's a nice head. A nicely shaped neck of a length that matches the rest of the pony and that meets the shoulder cleanly as mentioned above is a nice plus. Some people dislike a neck that comes too high out of the shoulder, feeling that it hampers free movement and prevents the pony from being able to stretch down and forward for the bit in dressage or as a show hunter. Others prefer them because the "uphill" pony is easier to balance for bigger fences or a higher degree of collection. A more uphill pony can also make some adult riders feel that there is a little more in front of their legs. Other people don't object to a heavier neck that comes lower out of the shoulder or that tends to a little crestiness. In either event, it should have a clean throatlatch and not be put on upside down, with the greater part of the muscling appearing to be on the bottom of the neck so that the pony can't go into the bridle easily when ridden. A correct shape helps make up for a slightly shorter neck, and a good shoulder will still give a nice length of rein to this mare or one whose withers are a bit flat. But especially in an older mare, be on the lookout for an overly cresty neck. While this is sometimes a trait that runs in families or one of the marks of a very fat pony, it can also point to the possibility of a hormonal imbalance that will hamper the mare's ability to be gotten in foal or to carry a pregnancy to term.

If everything else about a mare merits her becoming a good breeding prospect, the effects of living with a head that's a tad plain, or with bone that's a little light or a little coarse, or a back that could be shorter, or a croup that could be a bit more level, is not going to be life threatening. Any one of these problems *if it's minor* may be lessened by choosing only stallions to mate her with that are renowned for their lovely natures or feet or limbs or heads. But in a business already fraught with risk, it hardly seems worth the trouble to start out with too many concessions in basic conformation in the fond hope that some stallion will perform miracles.

SHE MAY BE PERFECT, BUT WILL SHE MAKE A BROODMARE?

Ideally, your foundation mare should not only be a superior individual with regard to conformation, she should also be as well bred as you can afford. This doesn't necessarily mean *popularly* bred. Fame and fads sway the world of pony breeding as erratically as they do any other, and this decade's hottest sire line could just as easily become the next decade's untouchable. But there is no question that certain families within any breed are known for passing on certain desirable traits. These may include superb movement, wonderful temperament, terrific bone and hardiness, great jumping ability, intelligence, and any number of other things. Similarly, there are certain stallions that, while they may never have become famous themselves, have demonstrated themselves to be consistently good sires of broodmares. A mare by one of these may well be a better long-term investment than one by this year's popular hero.

Good producers frequently run in families. If you find yourself consistently drawn to certain individual mares and fillies, a look at the tail female line will probably uncover either a common grandam or at the very least a common female ancestor in the fourth generation whose attributes have proven themselves to be very prepotent. Some study will show you which ones consistently pass on the traits you want. If you're in the position of buying a younger filly, try to get one from a mare that produces the kind of offspring you'd like to raise yourself. Always try to look at Granny, too—many breeders maintain that more often than not their foals resemble their grandparents more closely than they do their parents.

Another reason to buy fillies or maiden mares from proven female families is that many of the traits we most desire in our broodmares are nonquantifiable. The ideal broodmare is easy to breed, easy to settle, easy to carry, and easy to foal. She feeds her foals well and has good maternal instincts that include being protective of her foals without being overly aggressive toward her handlers. Thankfully, most mares enjoy raising their foals, but the equine world still has its share of mares with fertility problems and poor mothering skills. You won't know any of this about your chosen mare until she's actually produced a foal or two, but if you investigate her dam's and grandam's breeding histories and find no reproductive or behavioral problems, you'll probably be relatively safe.

A mare with a good competitive record will always be a strong selling point for her foals until a few of these are old enough to carry the torch for their siblings. These are frequently expensive, however, so the next best thing is to find the younger full or half sister of a mare whose performance record and family you admire. Although it can be frustrating having to wait the three years needed for a filly to mature to a sensible breeding age, you can use them to good advantage by taking her to the breed shows or showing her under saddle so that by the time you choose to retire her to the maternity ward she'll have some kind of record of her own.

It's sometimes possible to find an older mare whose owner has already kept some good daughters to carry on into the next generation of an established breeding program. When convincing the owner of the strength of your good intentions, it's helpful to have an idea of which stallions you'd like to send the mare to. Maybe you have access to one that the owner would have loved to use if it had been closer at hand. If you happen to own a very nice stallion yourself, another successful option is to lease the mare you covet for a certain number of breeding seasons, keeping one or two foals yourself and returning the mare to her owner in foal.

In the Thoroughbred industry, entire books are devoted to the nicking patterns of certain families of racehorses and how they translate into performance records. Nothing of this sort exists in the world of ponies, but it's nonetheless true that certain crosses work far better than others. The widespread use of transported semen has made it possible for many small breeders to create dream breedings that a few years ago would have been next to impossible. Still, if you intend to use one of several local stallions on your mares, it will pay you in the long run to find broodmare prospects that are related to mares that you *know* from observation and experience have nicked exceptionally well with that stallion. If you intend to raise crossbreds, use mares from a breed or cross that have succeeded well with him, too.

If you feel confident in your instinct that something else will work, by all means take the occasional risk, but back it up with solid homework. The research involved may sound like it's more trouble than it's worth, but compared to the trouble you're going to put into breeding, feeding, foaling, handling, and marketing, it's peanuts. And there's nothing more discouraging than starting off with a big bang of enthusiasm and being faced a couple of year's worth of hard work down the road with trying to sell disappointing youngstock.

Finally, have your broodmare prospects thoroughly vetted, not only for basic soundness and freedom from disease, but for any breeding problems that might be in the offing. A rectal exam will make sure that her reproductive tract and ovaries feel normal for her age and stage of development. In an older mare that's been bred before, a clean uterine culture is a must, and a uterine biopsy strongly recommended. Nothing is more discouraging than trying to get a nice mare bred, only to discover that the mare's uterus is so scarred from infection or foaling difficulties that her chances of maintaining a pregnancy are all but nonexistent. Try to get a complete medical and breeding history on the mare concerned to see whether she's had any problems showing heat, conceiving, or carrying a foal to term. All of these are legitimate concerns for any breeder, and necessary attributes for any broodmare.

Sometimes, despite your best information and experience, you're going to wind up with a mare that just plain doesn't work in your breeding program. When this happens, try to be realistic. Cut your losses and sell her. If you're like most small breeders—short on time, money, and space—a mare like this will be a constant financial and emotional drain.

There is a remarkable satisfaction in seeing a good mare's look stamped on her progeny, and in watching their talents unfold as they grow. The pleasure is made more intimate by the fact that each of your foundation mare's offspring is a limited edition. The better the foals are, the more credit the sire will probably get. But the breeder knows that the youngsters succeed because of the quality of the saintly mare in the back field. She'll prove her worth many times over the course of her life.

Learning to Assess Youngstock and Ponies in the Rough

Ponies are renowned for taking on unbelievably unattractive shapes and sizes before they reach any sort of stabilized maturity. You may look at a very promising and beautiful youngster that has a lot of good points one day, only to find a month later that it's gone completely coarse. You may look at another that you turn down as resembling nothing so much as a giraffe or a moose, only to find it's turned into a swan two years later—in somebody else's barn. Yearlings and two-year-olds may toe in one day, out the next, be cowhocked, have ears like mules, or no chest whatsoever. One week they may have rumps a hand taller than their withers. The next, no rear end at all and no withers either. The

A young pony turned out for showing is fairly easy to assess for conformation. *Photo: Connemara Country File.*

It's harder to pick one from a rough group in a field without a lot of studying of the frame underneath the fur and a sense of whether the youngster will grow out of (or into!) its awkward traits.

Sometimes, all you have to go on is the angles created by wither-to-point of shoulder-to-elbow, hip-to-point of buttock-to-stifle-to-hock, topline, and, of course, free movement. *Photo: Stan Phaneuf.*

yearling with a swanlike neck may grow into a two-year-old with a short, fat one. Will it revert? Is this the real animal? Who's to know? To make things worse, some youngsters may look absolutely perfect at two years, maturing into sausages by the age of five. Conversely, others may fool you completely by looking just fine at all ages.

Some horsepersons maintain that the ability to pick out good ones is inborn, and there are certainly a few blessed people in the world who seem to have an almost mystical sense of the future quality of a current clunker. But the rest of us mortals can learn how to see the elements that may combine to make tomorrow's champion.

The one single thing that will make your job easier is
a solid knowledge of how other members of the same
family have grown. A certain stallion may generally
pass on wonderful square hocks, for instance. Or a
broodmare may give most of her offspring a lovely
length of stride. Looking at the siblings and half siblings of the youngster that interests you is the best
measure of how consistently these are bequeathed to
various offspring. And by looking at relatives at various
different ages and stages of growth may give you a
sense of how a certain line of ponies matures. If they
tend to grow "all of a piece" and the youngster you're
examining has legs pointing in all directions, no chest,
and crooked hocks, you may be looking at the family's
token weed. If, however, this particular line is notoriously slow to develop, and all the yearlings you've seen
by the same sire tend to share these revolting traits
before becoming beautifully mature five year olds, you
could be looking at just another immature family member with great potential.

It's generally wise to give any young pony the benefit
of a little room to grow. A yearling or two-year-old that
already looks mature or is on the "stuffy" side is likely
to grow into something that is overly heavy or coarse
in another several years. Even those that grow in a consistent fashion ought to be a little on the rangy side to
give the idea that they have something to grow into. A
gangly colt with a big frame has a good chance of filling out that frame, in time and with the proper care
and work.

Although chests and hindquarters can broaden somewhat with age, necks can be developed, and heads and
ears grown into, some things are going to be pretty
much set in stone in youngstock. You're going to be
stuck with the shoulder angles you're looking at, and
with the length of croup and back. Slight cowhocks,
and even slight sickle hocks, may straighten themselves

with age and exercise. A goose rump will merely become a better-muscled goose rump. You're also stuck with bad feet or crooked legs, and although corrective measures can improve them in a potential performer, this is a bad idea in a breeding prospect. Correction is man-made. The tendency to poorly made limbs and feet is genetic. It will still be passed on to a certain number of a potential stallion or broodmare's future offspring.

In terms of fertility, a young, immature pony will not be able to be proven as a sire or a broodmare for a couple of years. When vetting them out, the most that you can really do is to try to get a complete medical history in order to rule out any history of illness, fever, or congenital problem that might affect future fertility, make sure that it is completely sound (a young pony in a healthy environment has no excuse for blemishes or any tendency to lameness), and ensure that its reproductive organs are maturing normally.

Ponies in the rough present potential buyers with a quite similar set of challenges.

We are all attracted by ponies that are fat, shiny, nicely turned out, and obviously well cared for. We tend to write off those that are hairy, unkempt, thin, or unhandled. It's no accident that ponies meeting the former criteria make better prices, both at the sales and from the breeding farm. A well-maintained and immaculately turned out pony fools the observer's eye into thinking immediately, "Wow! Beautiful!" even though a second, harder look may point up a variety of conformational defects that may range from a long back to a straight shoulder to legs that are something less than perfectly straight to a neck that is really not very attractively shaped.

In a thin pony, all of these flaws are immediately evident. It's the good qualities that are harder to ascertain. For instance, is the back really too long, and is the pony herring gutted? Or is this a function of being severely underweight and malnourished? Are the legs really crooked and the feet really cracked as well as ragged, or is this a matter of being trimmed correctly? Is that a ewe neck, or simply an unmuscled one? And what would the hindquarters look like after a few months of proper feeding combined with lunging or riding?

The trick here is to try to differentiate between those things that are the result of musculature (which can be changed drastically through feed, care, and exercise) and those that are structural (which is largely a question of bones). A perfect example of the latter would be the width of the chest and the shape of the legs. Width of chest is dictated by the way the ribcage is sprung and by the distance between the points of the shoulder. Although a very thin pony may appear narrower than a fat one due to the lack of flesh covering its ribs, all the good food and exercise in the world won't broaden a mature pony's chest much, because it's limited by skeletal structure. The situation is similar with legs, which derive their anatomy almost entirely from bone and the tendons and ligaments that cover them. Bench knees, calf knees, and cannons that are tied in below the knee or that rotate from knee to fetlock in a manner that makes toeing in or out a function of crooked limbs (rather than a foot imbalance created by inadequate farrier attention) will not improve. You're stuck with what you see. Cowhocks, a goose rump, and a very long back are also structural, but extra weight can make a back appear shorter, and the muscling that comes from consistent proper training can improve the appearance of both hocks and hindquarters. It won't make them go away, however, nor will it make them less heritable.

An overly fat pony, on the other hand, can disguise what might turn out to be a perfectly adequate shoulder angle and wither. Fat can make a pony look mutton-shouldered and cresty when in fact it might be

THE BREEDER'S CHECKLIST

The following points are listed in the order of importance most commonly assigned to them. To fine-tune it to your particular situation, you can give each point a numerical scale from one to ten when judging the qualities of potential broodstock.

1. Breed type

2. Conformation

3. Movement

4. Disposition (temperament)

5. Masculinity/Femininity

6. Bloodlines

7. Show record

8. Color

When assessing breeding stock for a crossbred program, these criteria will be somewhat different, and may look more like this:

1. Movement

2. Conformation

3. Show record

4. Disposition (temperament)

In this instance, breed type is not as important as overall quality and movement has been stressed more highly than conformation. There are reasons for this. First, it's rare that a pony of good breed type, correct limbs, and good movement will be badly conformed. Second, if your end product is to be a pony that has the capacity to be a superior performer, it must show athletic potential in the way it moves. But if it is to be good breeding stock, it must first of all be square.

perfectly fine with a hundred fewer pounds on its frame. At least the thin pony will show you what you've got in the structural sense—too much fat can hide some good qualities, as well as a multitude of faults.

That strange-looking neck might be improved immeasurably by work and a strict diet, as long as it isn't too coarse through the throatlatch and comes out of the shoulder in a way that looks like it might be clean.

Feet can be difficult. If you're looking at a pony that has never had adequate foot care, the question will always be whether the deviations that exist are natural or environmental. There is no easy answer for this. Studies have shown that mustangs in the wild wear their feet ragged, short, and healthy—but not necessarily straight—according to their various limb structures. When trimmed, these feet have been shown to be hard, round, and very sound. In a natural state on native soil, this is largely true of most pony breeds as well. In a domestic situation it's a little harder to judge. When looking at a rough pony with ragged-looking, long, or cracked feet, it would be wise to have a farrier whose opinion you respect highly try to evaluate the basic soundness of the foot and its structures, and whether proper trimming will yield up a pony that is sound and able to move squarely and in balance.

Trying to add or subtract weight mentally as you look at these ponies, and imagining them in work, shed out, trimmed, or even braided, isn't always easy in the face of the evidence standing in front of you. I once received the surprise of my life on taking a big, clunky mare that I'd bought as a broodmare to her first hunter show after many months of reschooling and a campaign to reduce her vast bulk by about half. Once she was all braided and working around the warm-up ring I realized that she'd become a very striking animal indeed. I'd just gotten used to thinking of her as a dumpling and hadn't noticed the profound changes she'd undergone until she was in a new context. She went on to be a handsome and very successful hunter, which made up for the fact that she turned out to be a bust as a broodmare.

The help of someone known for an ability to pick ponies in the rough and turn them into respectable breeding and performance stock is immensely valuable. This person will be able to explain to you why a certain pony that might look utterly hopeless to the casual eye has the potential to develop into something nice, while one you believe to be prettier might be passed over. With time, experience, and practice, your own eye will become more attuned to what exists underneath a coat of winter hair, two hundred extra pounds, a case of obvious malnutrition, or even what potential might reside within the body of the ugliest yearling you ever laid eyes on.

Chapter

7

CONSIDERING STALLIONS

If you're considering becoming the owner of a pony
stallion, there are two vital questions to ask yourself. First: *Am
I really prepared to deal with a stallion?* Most of the pony breeds
have justly earned their reputations for having exceptionally
tractable stallions, and it's quite common to see them safely ridden at home and in competition by experienced children as well
as adults. But even the nicest pony stallion is going to go through
periods of being noisy, egocentric, inattentive, macho, and opinionated. It's the nature of the beast to announce his presence
loudly whenever he arrives someplace new, and to strut, prance,
and generally let the world (or at least every other pony within
earshot) know what a tough and sexy guy he is. He will certainly
periodically test his limits with even his favorite people just to see
if he might be able to gain the upper hand. And he may be likely,
when in a clinic or competitive situation, to decide suddenly that
all the other animals in his class or in the warm-up area are his
own personal herd and be balky about leaving them. The stallion
handler must thus be a person who has an advanced sense of
humor—how else are you going to deal with the hunter class that
got blown when that cute grey mare walked across his field
of vision just as the last fence was coming up? The stallion handler must also have an acute knowledge of when discipline is

Most pony stallions have justly earned their reputations as tractable and easy to deal with. Here, Turkdean Sword Dance takes owner-breeder Hope Garland Ingersoll for a spin. *Photo: Bunny Ramsay.*

required, how much is called for, and how often it must be administered.

The most successful stallion handlers are those who are quiet, consistent, firm, and good-natured. They don't allow their egos to be wrapped up in those of their ponies, thus avoiding either a constant battle of wills between a resentful stallion and a handler determined to "show him who's boss" or the equally unpleasant sight of a handler allowing a stallion to get away with all sorts of rank behavior as if to demonstrate his (or her) ability to deal with such a difficult animal.

Once lost, the attention and respect of a mature stallion are notoriously hard to reestablish. Life with one is thus a little like being a judge who is expected every hour to behave in a moderated, well thought, and just manner. It requires a rock-solid consistency that even seasoned professionals often find daunting. Many won't have a stallion on their premises, good mannered or no. Stallions simply require too much attention and too much work to fit into most people's lives and barns comfortably.

On the other hand, a pony stallion that is happy with his life and with his people is a pony that will go anywhere and do anything you ask. They seem to have an inborn sense of loyalty and fairness that permits them to bond deeply with their people, and they are bold, fun, clever, sensitive, and never, ever boring.

The next question, then, is: *Why do I want a stallion?* The current ease of breeding mares artificially via transported semen enables most of us to use ponies that a few years ago would have been completely out of reach. Rather than buying your dream stallion and importing him from some other area at vast expense or using the less-than-ideal pony in the next town just because he's easy and within your price range, you can (with forethought and planning) run your whole breeding operation via Federal Express or UPS these days, and get exactly the mates you most want for your mares. Then if the foals don't live up to your expectation you aren't stuck with trying to sell the stallion and finding a new one that will suit your needs better.

ADVANTAGES TO OWNING

There are, however, still areas of the country where collecting, shipping, and receiving transported semen is a major production. And getting all your mares cycling for ease of insemination can be a problem in itself, especially since some mares ovulate sooner and off of different-sized follicles than others. In some situations feeding a stallion can work out to be cheaper than having a vet on call every other day to palpate and finally inseminate a group of mares.

Owning a stallion can sometimes also be a good move from a business and marketing standpoint. In the breeding business, it's stallions that get all the press, simply by merit of the number of offspring they can get on the ground every year. If you can turn a stallion out well and compete with him, as well as using him to breed, he can be a good drawing card for your farm. If he's successful—and you have the time, space, and flexibility to deal with outside mares—board and stud fees can be a handy way to help keep your farm in the black.

Before you start multiplying a hefty stud fee times forty mares a year, however, a word of caution is in order. Very few stallions actually get more than half a dozen outside mares in a year, and a lot of them get fewer than that. If you want to stand a stallion, you're far better off to have him because you feel he will be an asset to *your own* breeding program. He will be an asset either because he has an exceptionally hard-to-find bloodline that you want to save or that in your experience nicks ideally with your own mares; because he has certain traits of temperament, conformation, or movement that you want to use to improve the quality of your youngstock; or because the number of mares you own and breed makes owning a stallion more economical than paying stud fees and either board or collection fees to other farms.

FINDING "MR. RIGHT"

The most beautiful, or the most winning, or the biggest stallion you know is not necessarily going to be the one that will work best *with your mares*. No matter how good a stallion is in competition, and no matter how successful a sire he's been for others, he may not be suitable for the things that you most need.

Before committing yourself to a stallion, then, take an honest look at your mares. Could they use more bone and substance, or are they not as square behind as they might be? Then you'll need a stallion closer to the "old-fashioned" models that are still found on their native soils. Conversely, are they a little on the coarse or heavy side? Then you can safely introduce a stallion with a little more refinement. Do your mares have backs the length of California? Length is certainly a tendency in all pony breeds, and not a fault if kept within reasonable limits. But if "dachshund" is the first thing that crosses your mind when you look at your broodmares, find a mate that is shorter coupled. Could your ponies benefit from better movement? Look for a stallion with a very free shoulder and active hocks. These will give you plenty of stride when you ask for it.

An expressive head and kind eye are a great indication of temperament, as illustrated by Connemara *Rosenaharley Laurens (Rosenaharley Cormac x Leam Laurella). *Photo: Wade Alexander.*

A well-constructed and sound rear end is especially vital in a breeding stallion. This is where the power comes from, after all, and the ability to get over the big fences or push off into real collection. And the breeding process puts a tremendous amount of wear and tear on stifles and hocks, over time. The better conformed your prospect is at the start, the longer he's likely to stay sound and able to do his job.

Ponies are noted for their even temperaments, even though they can still be mischievous (stemming from that combination of intelligence and humor commonly known as the "pony mind"). Any sign of meanness or intractability or untrustworthiness should be enough to turn you off of a stallion, even if his conformation is the best you've ever seen. *Temperament is highly heritable.* Any professional who has worked with members of various equine families for any length of time will be able to tell you very accurately exactly what kind of nature you can expect from the

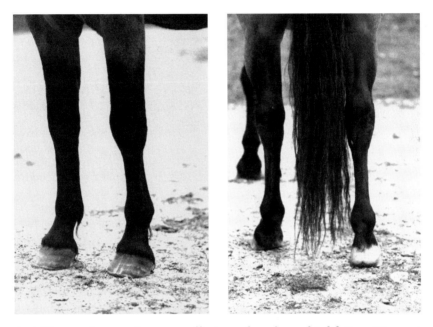

A stallion can have an immense effect on a breed over his lifetime. He must be absolutely correct, and have a hock and stifle configuration that will allow him to stay sound through the physical stresses of breeding. This pony beautifully illustrates the term "four square."

offspring of certain sires. Try to find one that people will come to because they like his reputation as a sane sire of sane ponies.

You can tell a lot about temperament by looking at a pony's eyes. They should be large and liquid. They will certainly be alert, if he's a self-respecting stallion, but they shouldn't give you the creepy sense that you wouldn't dare turn your back on him for a second. When you handle him and make reasonable requests about picking up feet, moving around, and leading, he shouldn't show any sign of resentment. If you're an unknown person to him, he may certainly try to nip or shove you to see if you're serious. A sharp word or tap should be enough to remind him that you're in control. If it isn't, and you spend your entire first look at him struggling to get him to stand still, pay attention, or stop biting, he will probably not be the kind of animal you want to deal with.

A good stallion will stamp his get with a certain predictable set of qualities. This attractive trio is clearly by the same sire. *Photo: Bunny Ramsey.*

The exception to this *may* be (but isn't always) a stallion that has had poor (if any) handling, or a yearling just learning manners. Again, look at the eye. Is it large and soft? Does it have an essentially kind expression? Does his nature seem to be basically nice and his actions a product of greenness or bad handling? If you're looking at a mature stallion, try to see how he behaves with his mares. Avoid a pony that is in any way savage or that seems to think that guerrilla tactics are called for in teasing and breeding. These are a recipe for certain injury to yourself, the stallion, and the mare, depending on who gets in the way first. Breeding manners can be taught, but they are also an extension of temperament.

Your stallion prospect *must* have straight limbs, excellent substance, and hard feet. These are attributes you expect to find in all pony breeds, and your stallion should exemplify them. Look at short cannons with lots of dense, flat bone. Look for feet that all match in size and shape, and that are not too steep and blocky. When you stand in front of him, make sure the stallion prospect's knees, cannons, and feet are all facing you rather than pointing in various different directions. If somebody says a pony is foursquare, that's what they mean.

Remember that although you are buying *one* stallion, you are investing in *all* of his offspring. A stallion can influence a breed very quickly over a short period of time. It's crucial, then, that stallions epitomize the very best of that breed's qualities. There are those who maintain that only 10 percent of all colts born deserve to be kept as stallions. You may or may not agree with this. You may decide that you can overlook some minor faults to get some other major qualities; or you may choose occasionally to maintain a less-than-ideal stallion in order to preserve a rare or unusual bloodline that is in danger of dying out but whose existence will over time be beneficial to a whole breed. These grey areas are where your knowledge, instinct, and research into inherited tendencies will pay off.

If you're buying a mature pony, you can look at a number of his offspring to see whether he consistently throws his strong points, whether he sires individuals that are better than himself, or whether his offspring are never quite as good as he is. When buying a colt, try to find one whose sire is noted for consistently passing on the characteristics you most desire. Pedigree study will further show how well your prospect nicks with mares that are bred similarly to yours.

THE REPRODUCTIVE EXAM

A reproductive exam is essential to make sure that your stallion prospect is sound for breeding and free from any aberrations that will affect his ability to sire offspring. Obviously, the pony must have two descended testicles. Cryptorchidism, or having only one testicle in evidence while the other is retained somewhere in the body cavity, doesn't necessarily adversely affect fertility. In some cases it can be repaired surgically, and the other testicle brought down. *But a cryptorchid should not be considered as a possibility for any breeding program under any circumstances*, as it is also a highly heritable condition that has no redeeming value.

A pony of breeding age should be collected to have its semen evaluated for viability, vigor, and freedom from deformities. Likewise, if you intend to use a stallion extensively for transported semen, it will behoove you to package a collected ejaculate to see how well it survives the collection and storage process. This is highly individual among stallions, and you shouldn't

In assessing movement, remember that each breed will have action specific to its type, as demonstrated here by Welsh Pony Barlys Troi of Penrhyn, Welsh Section D Cob Nesscliffe Sunrise, and Connemara *Chiltern Colm. Freedom of movement is vital, and powerful action from the hind legs (which creates impulsion and fuels stride, adjustability, and jumping ability) cannot be overestimated. The longest, prettiest front leg movement in the world is useless to you unless the hind legs back it up. *Photos: Bunny Ramsay, Toni Mayr, Stan Phaneuf.*

assume that the one you're looking at will ship well. This is doubly true when speaking of frozen semen, which varies greatly in its tolerances from one pony to another.

In older stallions, the viability of sperm is a definite concern, as virility sometimes declines with advancing years. Also important is the presence of arthritis in the hocks or stifles. Any breeding stallion that has been used heavily may be expected to get a little stiff with age; it's a job that entails a tremendous amount of wear and tear on the joints of the rear end. The question is whether his stiffness keeps him from being able to mount and stay on his mares comfortably. If his limbs aren't up to the job of getting him there, it won't matter how virile the pony is otherwise. Of course there are ways to collect older, unsound stallions from a standing position, but this is generally beyond the scope of the small breeder whose time and budget are already strained.

THE LEASING OPTION

If you're undecided about whether a stallion will fit into your life or whether he'll nick well with your mares, it's often possible to lease an older one for several years, especially if you can stand him in an area where he hasn't been used much. A nice mature pony stallion with good manners, a decent performance record, and plenty of breeding experience can teach the novice stallion handler a great deal that will be helpful when buying and schooling a colt later. It also gives you the potential of trying out several different stallions (if you can find them and persuade their owners to part with them) over a period of years. This allows you to see what nicks really work best for your mares as well as maintaining a broader gene pool, which may stand you in good stead in future generations. Owning a stallion and then finding yourself in the position of having to sell him (or lease him out) because you have nothing left to breed him to can be frustrating.

In leasing, make sure that you're very clear about who takes care of what, and for how long. Are you splitting breeding fees with the owner, or do you keep them all? Will you be responsible

A bold presence is part of any stallion's nature. He must still be mannerly in hand. Turkdean Sword Dance.

for all the stallion's bills? If not, which are exempt? Who pays for the insurance? How much should it be? And what other duties will the stallion be used for besides breeding? Answering all of these questions in contract form will protect both you and the pony's owner from the misunderstandings that can and do occur if you leave anything vague.

Standing a breeding stallion isn't an occupation for the totally uninitiated. Knowledge, experience, and a mannerly pony

115

A mannerly stallion that enjoys his work is a pleasure to work with, as shown by Connemara Hideaway's Erin Smithereen (*Tooreen Laddie x Erinbay) with owner-breeder Edward Harris. *Photo courtesy Hideaway Farm.*

are a must if you want to reduce the possible dangers and inconsistencies inherent in the process of owning and handling one. If you can, find an established breeder who you respect that will let you watch/help/learn through a breeding season so you'll know what to expect and how to go about it. Most universities and equine research centers also provide excellent courses for novice breeders. Take every opportunity to learn more.

The Stallion in Competition

A talented stallion that can keep his mind on the job at hand long enough to do well in performance is a real asset to his breed, as well as being your best possible advertisement until his get are old enough to do the job for him. The added competitive spark that a stallion's hormones give him also makes him brilliant and charismatic in the ring, whether jumping, driving, or in dressage.

On the other hand, there is nothing more frightening or disruptive than a barely contained, overexcited stallion trumpeting his way around a showground or wreaking havoc in the ring. Although most of us occasionally school green mares and geldings at shows perfectly safely, a stallion's behavior must be impeccable in hand, under saddle, and in company before you even contemplate taking him out in public. If you find him difficult to manage at home, he will be impossible at a show or event. The old tricks of putting Vicks in his nostrils to kill the scent of mares or using a stallion ring (a rubber ring designed to slip over the end of the penis to prevent a stallion from becoming erect in inappropriate moments) are no trade-off for simple good manners. No matter that you're certain of your ability to keep him under control when he's rank or unruly; neither his behavior nor your irresponsibility in insisting on inflicting his presence on others will be easily forgotten by show management, other competitors, or the owners of potential outside mares.

The three watchwords in competing with a stallion are always Safety, Safety, and Safety. No, it cannot be repeated too often. It relates not only to the safety of other ponies, riders, and spectators, but also to the safety of you and your stallion. This is a matter of planning and attention to detail as well as one of training.

When planning to show a stallion, always try to get stabling in permanent stalls. Stallions love to rub and push and roll and test to the limit the strength of their stalls. Most temporary stabling isn't up to that kind of treatment, no matter what the management says. If you contact them about your intent to bring a stallion to their show well in advance of their closing dates, you will usually find them very willing to accommodate your request for permanent stabling or for a corner stall, where your stallion can be quieter and less pressed by other ponies. Failing a corner, try to arrange to have a tack stall or a quiet gelding beside and behind him. And always bring a couple of web stall guards or a full metal screen to put over the top of the stall door. Remember that even a very tractable stallion is likely to become territorial and excited when surrounded by dozens of other horses and ponies. It's a rare owner that doesn't have at least one horror story to tell about a stallion spending entire twenty-four hour periods on his hindlegs trying to peer into the stalls adjoining his, or attempting to leap over (or crawl under) stall doors to investigate the interesting mares going by, or even kicking down the boards between stalls to get into the one next door. Don't think for a moment that your pony would never do such a thing. Assume that he will and arrive prepared, even when you've trained him to be mannerly in all situations. If he remembers all you've taught him when he gets to the showground, you can congratulate yourself and smugly accept the admiration of passersby who never knew that stallions could be so well behaved.

When riding a stallion in a group, remember that nobody is going to make concessions for you. Most riders are entirely ignorant of what can happen if they crowd a stallion, and very quick to blame you for the consequences, even if the fault was theirs. You as the rider must have eyes everywhere and total concentration. It's up to you to make sure that situations don't get out of hand. Try, therefore, to keep your stallion on the perimeters of crowded areas, avoiding them altogether if he's tense and needs a lot of quiet work to warm up. When hacking, keep him wherever he's safest, whether this means a little off the rail, or traveling through the deep spot that everybody else is avoiding, or floating a little to the outside of the crowd. This may mean you won't be as visible to the judge, but your first consideration must be safety.

Between classes, take him off to a relatively quiet spot rather than insisting that he stand in the middle of a crowded warm-up area while you chat with your friends. Demanding good manners is one thing, inviting trouble quite another. Even if your pony is dead quiet, somebody else's mare may take exception to his existence and back halfway across the ring for the pleasure of kicking him. And if another pony takes a pot shot at him, or crowds him, or nickers an invitation to him, he's going to respond. It's just his nature. Walking or standing at a small distance from the throng will allow him to watch everything, which will make him happy, but keep him out of harm's way. It's lonelier for you, but infinitely more courteous to your fellow competitors.

The most important rule after safety is that you cannot fall off. Ever. Thinking of the chaos that would result if they ever got dumped by their stallions has given many a rider both nightmares and incredibly tight positions.

It's very rare that a pony stallion will be as consistent in performance as a gelding or a mare. Even the best of them will have days when the distractions are too overwhelming, especially early in the season when they're still covering mares at home. But the examples of breeding stallions who successfully combine careers are numerous. If you take the time to develop your pony, there's no reason why he can't do both and be a great ambassador to his breed and to your farm.

Chapter

FEEDING AND HOUSING
THE PONY

Perhaps the most damaging myths that surround ponies are those concerning their care. True believers of every breed are known to make a variety of proclamations which may include that their ponies keep on air and rarely need shoes, even in work; thrive on rough feed (like gorse, furze, seaweed, even in a pinch dead fish, and other such essentially prickly and/or unpalatable substances); and rarely need any veterinary attention. These statements are meant as a comparison with other horses whose needs are much more labor- and cash-intensive, and are certainly descriptive of the poverty-stricken circumstances in which many pony breeds evolved. In the hands of the uneducated, however, they have been responsible for untold misery to ponies whose new owners took them at face value.

There is a vast difference between the words *survive*, which most ponies can manage to do for a period of time in some pretty horrible surroundings, and *thrive*, which no pony can do without adequate feed and care. The truth is that ponies starve to death, get colic, pick up internal parasites, and go lame just as often as horses do if basic keep and health-care requirements are not met. Those who point out the conditions under which many pony breeds subsist in their native settings must also agree that most of these ponies look pretty poor at the end of a long winter if left to fend for themselves, and that many of them do in fact die.

Yet it's also a mistake to believe that ponies must have the same level of care that horses do in order to thrive. Ponies' metabolisms are different than those of larger horses. The way their systems have evolved to handle climatic extremes and use the various nutrients found in low-powered feeds has been very specific. If we were to feed a pony according to the weight requirements suggested by grain manufacturers for the "average" horse, we would either founder the pony or create a monster too hot to be ridden by anybody but a skilled professional. The lush pasture that is recommended for Thoroughbreds is death to many ponies. And where shelter is concerned, ponies are much happier and more tractable if allowed to live outside (or as near to it as possible) for the better part of their lives. Their relatively thick, coarse coats provide natural weather proofing in all but the worst situations, combined with their natural tendency to good feet and an essential freedom from some of the lamenesses and congenital defects that are present in certain horse breeds can make them practically trouble-free.

It can thus be reasonably stated that the needs of most ponies range from minimal to very moderate *when compared with the requirements of a larger hot-blooded (or even warm-blooded) horse*. But they still need:

1. Adequate feed and free access to water.

2. Adequate shelter from extremes of heat, cold, sleet, bugs, etc.

3. Routine vet care, including a good rotational deworming program.

4. Routine care from a farrier.

This chapter covers the first two items. The third and fourth elements listed will be covered in Chapter 9.

FEED: FROM FORAGE TO SUPPLEMENTS

Recent research has brought to light an extraordinary amount of valuable technical knowledge about total digestible nutrients, grams and milligrams of vitamins and minerals that you never knew existed, and minute measurements of trace elements. This information has made it easier than ever before to pinpoint exactly what it is that any equine requires to thrive whether breeding, lactating, jumping, trail riding, or simply standing around. It has also given rise to the marketing of a staggering number of supplements, additives, and grain rations all purporting to meet these needs better than those of their competitors.

The four most vital elements in feeding your ponies properly are still pretty basic: good pasture, good hay, free access to salt, and plenty of fresh water.

Pasture and Hay

The term *good pasture* doesn't have to be synonymous with "rich" or "lush" pasture. In general, ponies do better on a mixed pasture than they do on anything overly rich that may founder them, and in many cases decent grass may be all they require to thrive for most of the year. This isn't to say that an old weedy field grown over with mustard and goldenrod is going to do them any good. A good broad mix of grasses such as timothy, redtop, orchard-grass, etc., when combined with red and white clovers, trefoil, or some alfalfas, makes an excellent forage combination either as pasture or as hay for ponies in all stages of life and work. This mix will of course vary according to the climate and growing conditions that exist in various parts of the country. Your county cooperative extension service will be able to provide you with suggestions on judging what will do best for your ponies, but it's up to you as a breeder to know what you're after in terms of an overall pasture mix.

Even among ponies, feed requirements can vary greatly according to whether you're pasturing broodmares, youngstock,

An overgrazed, weed-infested pasture is no good to anybody.

performers, or a combination of all three. It's important to know, for instance, that certain fescues that are perfectly adequate forage for nonbreeding animals have been proven to be abortogenic in some bred mares. Equally important is the knowledge that a pasture too rich in legumes is potentially harmful to ponies. You want a good mixed pasture heavy on permanent grasses for easy keeping ponies who don't require a huge level of protein or a rich concentrated diet. Information like this will be of inestimable help to your advisers when it comes to developing a good plan.

Like any tool, your pasture is going to require maintenance to keep it at its optimum level of production. Ponies (and horses) are not the most complete grazers in the world, and will choose to range over a pasture eating the most tender and delectable shoots first while stamping or manuring on the rest and wasting a great deal of less-interesting but equally nutritious feed. In a natural system, groups of browsing ponies could range over thousands of acres nibbling at will without returning to an old grazing ground until adequate regrowth had occurred. In this system, they are also aided by the additional grazing of various other herbivorous types (sheep, goats, cattle, and their ilk) whose taste buds cause them to seek out different plants or different sections of plants. The whole effect is one of stimulation of plant growth, the propagation of beneficial species through adequate rest periods, and enough forage for all as long as the population remains balanced.

Unfortunately, we can rarely imitate this system in our pasturing of ponies. Most of us don't have access to unlimited acreage, nor do we keep sheep or cattle as well as equines. And rather than giving our fields any rest period, we tend to turn our ponies out on permanent pasture in the spring (when there is usually more rich growth than they can handle efficiently or safely) and leave them there until the ground freezes or is covered with snow. The ponies range selectively, as always, returning over and over again to favored plants. When these are eaten down to the point that they no longer have enough leaves to photosynthesize, the plants wear out and stop growing back. This gives various ranker grasses and weeds a chance to crowd in and take over, not to mention ordinarily unpalatable toxic plants that ponies may start nibbling on if all else fails. The eventual result of the cycle is the kind of weed-infested, overgrown field that is a common sight on any rural road, and the strong possibility of a pony falling ill from eating the wrong plant because nothing else was left.

Proper rotation to rest pastures, mowing annual weeds and rank grasses, and dragging to break up manure piles can encourage good growth throughout the grazing season.

Of course you can renovate your pastures every few years and start over again, but that route is both costly and time consuming. Maintenance is cheaper, and begins with having your farm's soil tested so that you know which nutrients are abundant and which are lacking. The test is easy. You simply take a sample of soil at an average depth of two inches from several different sections of your pastures, bag it up, and submit it to the cooperative extension service lab in your state to be analyzed. The analysis will let you know things like whether your fields require serious fertilization to replace nutrients lost over many years of abuse (potash and phosphorus levels are frequently low in these instances), and how much lime may be needed to bring the soil pH back up to a level that will support good growth.

Once you've attended to the overall fertility problems of your fields, general maintenance can usually be attained by a suitable rotation of pastures that allows regrowth of grasses and legumes to reach a level that will sustain a certain amount of regrazing. If your pastures aren't crossfenced to allow for rotation, the many highly portable electric fence systems now on the market can give you an easy and effective way of dividing pastures so that less feed is wasted through inefficient grazing, moving the ponies before overgrazing occurs (ideally, when the stubble is down to about two and a half inches, or whatever height allows enough leaves left over for photosynthesis to occur). The grazed section can be mowed to cut back any weed growth (weeds are usually annuals, so cutting them before they go to seed is a very effective way of controlling them), dragged to break up piles of manure, and left to rest. At the same time, you can walk through your pastures to pull up any toxic plants and eliminate them from the menu, as well as getting rid of any branches and limbs from trees containing poisonous substances that might have blown into the field during periods of bad weather or high winds. Lists and descriptions of toxic plants can be obtained from the extension service or your vet.

Optimum regrowth time will vary according to your region's climate, the season, and the way in which various grasses and legumes replenish themselves. Certain plants such as orchardgrass and birdsfoot trefoil can withstand reasonably heavy

125

use, and will recuperate fairly quickly. Alfalfa can only withstand about three to four days of steady grazing, requires twelve inches to fourteen inches of regrowth before it can safely be regrazed, and shouldn't be grazed early in the season until it has headed out, which may make it a poor bet for permanent pastures in most situations. Timothy and bromegrass also do better if allowed to head out before grazing.

If your acreage is small for the number of animals you keep, it's still possible to maintain a good pasture base by more intensive rotation, fertilizing, and renovation. You may also need to have a smaller paddock or two that can be used for certain parts of the day or in certain seasons to take the stress off of your fields while still allowing your ponies free exercise. You might think of this space as a "designated dead area," that is, one that is going to be used specifically as a holding area, schooling ring, or starvation paddock for fat ponies, rather than a place known for its ability to grow grass.

Ponies that can't graze all day or throughout the seasons for their feed will need hay to supplement their diets. The kind of mixed pasture that we've discussed also describes the kind of hay you'll be looking for. Straight alfalfa or other entirely legumous hays are really too rich for most ponies, and should be fed in moderation, if at all. In some areas of the country, good grass hays are difficult to find, but it's worth the effort. A pony's stomach is designed to digest small, steady amounts of roughage over a long period of time. Feeding them a great deal of richer food at widely spaced intervals not only runs the risk of overloading systems that are intolerant of too much high-powered fare, it also leads to the boredom that results in vices like chewing wood, cribbing, and the other assorted horrors that we spend hours trying to prevent. A good mixed hay from well-maintained fields can provide most of the nutrients needed by the average mature pony in light work, and serves the dual purpose of giving them something to do that doesn't involve reducing your barn to splinters.

Ponies, being notoriously greedy, will eat just about anything, including hay that really ought to be mulch. And they can just as easily die of it as their more fastidious horse-sized cousins. Whether you buy hay out of the field, from a dealer, or make it yourself, always check the quality of the bales you receive. Good hay is dry, free from dust or mold, and not too stalky. Look for plenty of grass heads or legume leaves, a fresh smell, and good color (light green in grass hays, darker green in legume hays). A good bale of hay when dropped will bounce a little. If it lands with a heavy, dead "thunk" when you drop it, shove your hand as far into the middle as you can and bring out a handful; chances are it'll be wet or moldy. Don't accept hay like this.

Ponies and Grain

Grain and *pony* are two words that must be used together with caution. There are certainly situations in which ponies require grain. A pony in moderate to heavy work may need extra calories to make up for the stressful environments of shows, trailering long distances, and busy barns. Broodmares with foals at foot, some youngstock, breeding stallions, and aged ponies will also benefit from some grain added to their diets. Oats are the most digestible and palatable feed for horses and ponies, and have a useful protein level of about 10 percent. More than that—along with too much heating feed like molasses, alfalfa cubes, corn, and the like—may create a supercharged and unmanageable monster. If you prefer a mixed feed or a pelleted ration, there are many choices now available with the right protein range, and they can be combined with oats to bring the total level down a bit if needed.

Young, fast-growing ponies may need the extra carbohydrate offered in a mixed grain, but again, the protein level should be monitored carefully. The tendency among market breeders who show their youngstock is to push high-calorie, high-protein feed at their youngsters in the interest of producing ponies that are large and fat. *This is not necessarily healthy.* A fat yearling growing beyond its natural capacities puts a tremendous strain on immature joints and tendons, which are not capable of carrying great weights or of stretching beyond a certain point without sustaining some level of damage. Feed that's too rich can all too easily create other lasting problems, as well. Two of the most common are osteocondritis dessicans, or OCD (a painful inflammation of the joints that can cause irreversible problems leading to lameness), and contracted tendons, which in severe cases can cause the pony's heels to be lifted right off the ground so that it looks as if it were walking on its toes. Sometimes this can be corrected surgically, but it's far simpler (and less expensive) to prevent it from the outset.

It should be noted that feeding the mare a diet that's too rich can also lead to a foal's contracting either condition. Shoving extra grain to your mare just because she's in foal or lactating is tricky. On one hand you need to make sure she gets the nutrition she needs to support her foals well; on the other you don't want to overdo it and risk damaging the foal. Mares will need little if any adjustment to their normal feed until the last three months of pregnancy, when the fetus goes through seven-eighths of its growth process. Then grain can be added carefully to maintain adequate weight without allowing mares to get too fat. After parturition, some pony mares (especially older ones) may need their feed doubled in order to maintain their foals properly without losing a great deal of weight. Others are extremely rich milkers and require very little supplementation to do very well by themselves and their foals. When added bulk is needed to maintain weight and condition in broodmares and youngstock without raising the overall protein/carbohydrate/fat level too greatly, beet pulp makes a good feed additive. This must be soaked before feeding, but it's inexpensive, is a good source of roughage, and in pelleted form is easy to handle and store.

Since ponies' feeding needs vary widely from one individual to another, it's nearly impossible to set out a feeding chart that will accurately feed a general population. Your vet can assist you in developing a solid feeding program. Again, a conservative approach is best, and as a general rule it's safer to add roughage before increasing the grain ration, even for ponies that are in heavy work. The most important thing, however, is to know your ponies as individuals, and be able to adjust your rations according to the combined "old-fashioned" indicators of condition, weight, temperament, and work.

Vitamins, Minerals, and Supplements

The last element in your feeding program is supplements. The most vital of these is salt, which is necessary to the survival of all mammals. Salt should be offered to all of your ponies at all times. They are the best monitors of when and how much they need, and if left access to it will take exactly what they need. Salt can be purchased in block or loose form either plain, mineralized with trace elements that are lacking in many soils, or iodized, depending on the needs of your specific region. When in doubt, your vet can recommend the variety to be offered, but as a general rule, a mineralized salt block offers what might be referred to as "cheap insurance" and should be the salt of choice in most cases.

Seventy percent of the minerals in a pony's body consist of calcium and phosphorus, which are essential to the formation and maintenance of normal bone and teeth. Although many feeds contain one or the other of these minerals naturally, the balance between them is critical. If either is too heavily concentrated, they'll bind together so that neither can be readily absorbed by the pony's system. The result of inadequate absorption is that the system will pull what it needs from bone reserves. This obviously spells trouble, especially for youngstock. Mature ponies can tolerate a calcium-to-phosphorus level of anywhere from 1:1 to 6:1, though the latter is far from ideal. Youngstock, however, require a much narrower 1:1 to 2:1 range to meet the huge needs of laying down adequate bone growth. Your vet can help you analyze whether your ponies need supplementation beyond that which is available in hay, grain, and mineralized salt. When in doubt, the addition of two to three ounces of dicalcium phosphate or a similar supplement can correct any insufficiency without going overboard or breaking the bank.

A regular grain ration can also be supplemented by adding an ounce or two of corn or peanut oil per day, which provides valuable fats as well as some vitamins (like vitamin E) that can improve coat and skin condition. The addition of oil can also be useful in very cold climates, where it provides the pony's system with extra fuel to keep warm. It should be noted again that

129

In some areas, keeping water from freezing faster than it can be used is a problem all winter. This system, which uses a bath-tub (all fittings removed) surrounded by rigid insulation and a plywood casing, provides open water for a much longer period of the day, and keeps it cooler in summer.

ponies need far less oil than horses do to maintain condition. The half-cup to cup of oil recommended for some horses can severely strain a pony's system. It's best to err on the side of caution and stay with a smaller amount unless *specifically* advised otherwise by your vet.

A serious deficiency in the essential combination of vitamin E and selenium has been linked with certain degenerative diseases in foals and young horses, notably equine degenerative myeloencephalopathy (EDM), a condition of the spinal cord that has been recognized as causing one form of wobbler's syndrome. Broodmares living in geographical areas known to be selenium-deficient may require supplementation of this critical combination throughout pregnancy to ensure the health of their foals. It should be noted, however, that while the requisite amount is necessary for health, an overdose of selenium is toxic. It should thus be fed only according to instructions, and only in conjunction with vitamin E, without which it can't be properly used by the system.

Commercial Cure-alls

Offering a feed supplement because "it can't hurt and might help" is both expensive and wasteful, no matter how great the testimonials to its effects may be. This is assuming that your ponies' needs are being met through the proper quantity and quality of forage, grain, water, and salt. Used properly, however, according to needs that you and your vet have agreed exist in certain of your ponies, and according to manufacturers' instructions, the proper supplement for a specific use in a specific pony or ponies can be a very beneficial addition to their health and well-being.

Water

Quite simply, water is *critical*. It must be fresh, it must be plentiful, and it must be available at all times. Water that is allowed to sit in the hot sun for too long, or that grows scum or has an oily film on it, or has not been changed frequently enough, will be totally unpalatable to ponies, and may even contain harmful elements that will make them sick if they finally drink it in desperation. The risk of letting ponies get dehydrated through neglect or because you forgot to go out to see if the stream was still running after the recent drought is great, and by the time it's noticeable to our eyes it can be far advanced. *Make sure that ample supplies of water always exist, free choice.* As with salt, the pony is the best arbiter of how much water it needs and how often it needs it. This amount will change from day to day according to weather, season, ground moisture, climate, whim, and a hundred other variables that you won't be able to predict. Don't even attempt to second-guess this—just provide the water.

SHELTER: FROM COAT TO CONSTRUCTION

By nature of their long and arduous evolution, ponies are generally fairly weatherproof. In winter, a thick coat is a wonderful insulator. Each hair shaft traps air around it so that the pony is essentially wrapped in a layer of warmth-retaining material that is as effective as the fiberglass in a well-insulated house's roof. The sight of a pony with a snowbank on its back, though it may chill us to the bone, is actually no cause for alarm. The fact that the snow hasn't melted is testimony to the adequacy of the pony's own furry insulation, and the snow actually adds to the warmth

Ponies' natural coats give them abundant protection in an extraordinary range of climates, as shown by Fjord Stina (Ene x Silja). *Photo: Carol Rivoire.*

being kept in. A pony among other "equine snowbanks" that is wet from melted snow is more like a leaky roof, and far more likely to be at risk for chilling. Likewise, those bushy manes and tails that are the bane of our existence when we're trying to pull or braid them serve an added purpose when the air is frigid, by protecting ears and eyes from sleet and snow and helping to shed precipitation. A bushy tail spread out against the wind when ponies are in that typical woebegone "end of the trail" stance in storms presents the broadest and most weatherproofed part of its anatomy to the worst of the wind, deflecting it from the vital organs and head.

In summer, the pony sheds its winter coat to a shorter, silkier one in just the same way that we take off our overcoats. Sweat aids the skin in cooling through evaporation, and helps to remove heat from surface veins that carry the somewhat cooled blood through the body. The same bushy mane and tail now do double duty as bug repellent and "screens" for head, ears, eyes, and face. And some specialists maintain that even the specific configuration of the whorls on a native pony's head and body serve an important function in directing water away from sensitive areas, just as rain gutters do for a house.

The added topography of hills, trees, hedges, and other natural windbreaks and shelters aid the pony's ability to protect itself from both cold and heat. Ponies have an unerring ability to seek out the one place in the whole field that is actually more out of the wind (in winter) or in the path of the only available breeze (in summer).

It would seem, then, that ponies are fine without extra shelter in most cases, and many excellent books about ponies written in the British Isles will maintain that this is so. It must be recognized, however, that this concept stems from a climate that is almost always moderate, and that is dependent on a constant supply of forage and water. It won't meet the needs of most pony breeders in North America, where almost every extreme of temperature can be found. The shelter needs of a pony in Ontario, Canada, will differ greatly from those of a pony in Southern California, and all of the climatic zones in between will come with individual peculiarities that require attention and some form of constructed shelter.

Northeastern winters, for instance, are notorious for winter storms that lash the region with freezing rain, wind, and sleet. Our normally weatherproof pony, even given its dense and oily coat, can't withstand this for very long before becoming wet through. Once wet, the coat can't keep the pony warm, and chilling is a very real danger. Further, in northern climates that commonly have as much as six months of subfreezing (and frequent subzero) temperatures accompanied by a heavy snow load, any available forage dies back and leaves literally nothing for a pony to eat. And although ponies can and will eat snow for moisture, it doesn't supply anywhere near enough water to maintain health, and the internal BTUs required to melt it rob a pony's system of valuable energy.

In summer or in very hot, dry climatic regions, water becomes a major problem. Another difficulty is access to adequate grazing during the long spells of drought that are a feature of many areas in the United States. Heatstroke is a real danger for dark-coated animals, especially among ponies whose general make-up includes skin and haircoat on the thick side and thus not genetically engineered to shed heat in the way that, say, an Arab can. Heavy, hot, humid air restricts the body's ability to cool through sweat, and recent studies have shown that without access to proper cooling as described above, internal organs can actually be severely damaged by "cooking." Further, a pony with the characteristic pink skin underneath white facial markings is very prone to sunburn and blistering. And bloodsucking, stinging insects in some areas are fierce, hungry, and too numerous to battle with just a mane and tail as defense.

Of Rugs and Sheets

The situations described above can sometimes be modified by the addition of the many available permutations of the famous New Zealand–style rug. The traditional form, which is canvas lined with wool and feels like it weighs about three hundred pounds, is one of the best added protections ever invented for ponies living in nasty winter climates. The canvas cover is virtually indestructible and highly water- and wind-resistant. The wool liner provides warmth (real wool maintains its ability to retain warmth even when wet) and another layer of insulation between pony and air. Leg straps keep the whole thing from shifting, so that a pony can be left out for a period of time without the worry of finding its rug ripped or hanging in festoons around the neck. Newer materials such as polar fleece as a liner and ballistic-strength nylon for covers have led to the creation of rugs that are just as durable and a fraction of the weight. In an emergency, a pony wearing one of these rugs can stay warm, dry, and toasty underneath, even when its head and neck are completely covered with icicles.

Summer protection can be given a boost by any one of a number of turnout sheets made of mesh and again reinforced with leg straps, nylon bindings, and so on. Advanced bug spray

Sheds can range from the cozy to the commodious. The third photograph shows a useful shed off the side of a barn, giving extra options.

formulas help to keep biting insects at bay temporarily, and in some parts of the country it isn't unusual to see entire pastures full of horses and ponies wearing net bug hats and looking for all the world like extraterrestrials. All of these tools become especially useful if you've removed your ponies' natural protection by clipping them, removing ear hair and whiskers, or pulling manes and tails in the interest of winter riding or summer showing.

The Run-in Shed

When talking of built shelters, a three sided run-in shed may turn out to be the most efficient, least labor intensive, and easiest form of shelter to maintain. In some states, they are also the law.

Sheds have a lot to recommend them. From the human standpoint, they offer the peace of mind of knowing that your ponies can get out of any kind of weather at will. From the pony's perspective, there is the pleasure of being able to choose when that might be. The old joke among horsepeople is that you'll find your ponies standing out in the middle of the field, snoozing through the worst blizzard of the year, while their warm, dry shed stands empty. But sheds will get plenty of use in soaking up January's weak sun, or recuperating from weeks of rotten weather, or fighting insects, or as a haven from a heat wave.

The siting, materials, and construction of a good shed will vary from region to region. A flat-roofed shed that is open-sided to maximize shade and air movement in the Southwest, for instance, would be entirely unsuitable for use in the Northeast, where three solid sides and a peaked roof to shed snow is a necessity. Before building, check with other breeders in the area to see what works best for them, and to see what your county extension office may have to say on the subject in terms of regional needs and state laws.

As a general rule, a run-in shed should face south, away from the prevailing wind and maximizing winter sunlight and heat. Size varies according to the numbers of ponies that will be using it, and whether or not they get along. Two or three buddies may be fine in a shed that measures 12 feet by 20 feet, but no shed will be large enough for sworn enemies. When in doubt, err on the side of roominess. Current recommendations suggest 150 square feet as an adequate measure for one horse; a bit less for a pony. In shape, it should be rectangular, substantially longer than it is deep. A small, deep shed will enable a pasture bully to pin a less bold pony to a back wall with no avenue of escape.

The Value of Barns

There are times when a real barn may be needed. If you're in the process of trying to civilize youngsters, boarding outside mares, showing a pony, or nursing a sick or lame one—or even if you prefer to keep your ponies in during the hottest summer days or coldest winter nights—a few enclosed stalls are very handy. Barn designs are almost as numerous as barns themselves, and range from the elegant simplicity of racetrack shed rows to the opulent show barns of leading show hunter stables. Some have commodious lofts that allow hay storage above the stalls, which is a nice way of providing added insulation. Others have separate buildings for this in consideration of fire regulations or efficiency. Some have separate foaling and observation stalls. Others allow these to be created through movable partitions. Flooring may be variously of wood, clay, stone dust, or rubber mats. Aisles may vary greatly in width, and "extras" may include a large selection of tack rooms, feed rooms, and offices. In some areas the best basic material may be stone and concrete, which are cool and easy to maintain. In others, wood may be preferred, being warmer and locally more available.

The main idea is to find what works best, most efficiently, and most economically for your individual needs and in your situation, and then build it; or adapt an existing structure to meet your specifications. Essentially, your structure must be rugged enough to withstand years of abuse by ponies that will from time to time try to eat it, pound it to a pulp, use it as a scratching post and percussion instrument, and dig holes in it. Wood walls will probably need some sort of metal strapping to reinforce chewable edges. Floors must be well drained to prevent the collection of moisture and ammonia fumes from urine, have good traction, and provide a warm and reasonably inviting surface to lie down

137

on. Aisles must be wide enough to get your machinery through and to have a pony comfortably crosstied in without running the risk of being chewed on by a neighbor. Stalls must be large enough to allow your ponies freedom of movement and the ability to lie down and have a good roll without instantly being cast. A good average is 10 feet by 12 feet.

Light and adequate ventilation are critical for health, and many structures are lacking in these important attributes. In most cases it isn't enough that doors and windows can be opened and closed to allow breezes through or to prevent howling gales from chilling everybody. Horses and ponies create a lot of heat simply by standing around and breathing, and barns build up a great deal of moisture through the condensation from many warm bodies, wash stalls, water tubs, and so on. All this moisture has to go somewhere, and most barns are woefully lacking in a way to get rid of it. The problem increases if you have an attached indoor arena where both ponies and people daily work up a good sweat, and barns and indoors alike have thus earned a reputation for being unbelievably damp in certain seasons. And bacteria and viruses thrive in the kind of warm, moist environment that exists in many barns that are kept closed up due to an overcautious attitude toward potential drafts.

This needn't be the case. Some excellent venting systems exist that are capable of carrying this moisture away rather than allowing it to be constantly recycled through the air. Cupolas are very effective, as are ridge and gable-end vents. But no system will work efficiently unless it has an air intake in the form of open doors or (since most barn owners like closing doors for various reasons) built-in soffit intake. This may sound like a lot of extra trouble, but it's far less than most people realize. The extra money spent on rooftop ventilation will more than pay for itself in the better health of your ponies and a longer life for your barn and equipment. And stabled ponies will thrive on as much fresh air as you can give them.

Finally, it pays to remember that a modest, well-maintained farm with nice-looking, beautifully kept stock and friendly operators will sell ponies just as well as the far grander structures that may exist in our wildest dreams.

Two common styles of fencing: slip board (with two strands of electric wire running inside it to keep ponies from leaning on it) and PVC (showing clip assembly on wooden posts).

Keeping Them Down on the Farm

Ponies love escaping. Some lift latches, some jump from place to place, some crawl under doors and fences, and others just wriggle through whatever small hole may have opened up in some obscure corner of the field. Finding a way to keep them in is essential.

139

There are more materials than ever before available for fencing, which gives a breeder plenty of options when investigating this all-important facet of pony-keeping. They range from traditional wood, to vinyl and PVC look-alikes, to both square and diamond mesh wire, to simple electric systems with one or two wires, to more complex systems with three or more strands and springs to hold tension. All of these materials have strengths as well as drawbacks. Wood is expensive, rots over a period of time if not maintained consistently, and runs the risk of being chewed by bored or ambitious ponies. The various petroleum-product derivatives are even more expensive, can suffer chemical breakdown from the abuses of sun and weathering, and require a great deal of care in the setting of corner posts strong enough to keep them from sagging. Mesh wire, even with a board along the top to keep ponies from leaning on it, can sag from the expansion and contraction induced by temperature extremes, also requires great care in its support and tensioning, and may rust over time. High-tensile electric systems, by far the most economical, can break when run through, and have the great disadvantage of being very difficult to see unless colored tape is used or unless ponies have learned to look for it from post to post (which they do, once they're accustomed to it). On the plus side, all provide good, safe methods of keeping your ponies where you want them when properly installed.

The type of fence you use is thus largely an individual question based on need, budget, aesthetics, the climate you live in, availability of materials, and the size of the area to be fenced.

One breeder may find it infinitely more economical in the long run to fence entirely with wood, while another will swear by any one of the other systems. Many people find that a combination may work best. You might want to have the traditional look of a wood fence in front of the property where it's highly visible, and prefer to use woven wire elsewhere. You may have had a lot of success with the excellent high-tensile electric fences, yet maintain a couple of vinyl-fenced paddocks for mares with young foals at foot or outside mares that haven't been accustomed to wire. Talk to people in your area who are using any or all of these various options to get a feel for how they might fit into your life.

Then prepare to spend a certain part of your life repairing it. In the long run, no fence is truly maintenance-free, and all will require some form of care in every season to make sure that they're still pony-tight. Rails break, corner posts lean, trees fall, bushes grow, and ponies test. It all adds up to a lot of wear and tear. As always in this business, early attention to small needs will largely eliminate far more costly replacements later on.

Addressing the Needs of Stallions

A stallion's life can be a pretty lonely one. Unless you have one who is turned out with his harem year 'round, he probably spends a great deal of his time by himself, which is not a happy situation for a gregarious herd creature. A working stallion may be kept happy by the grooming and attention he gets every day, as well as by the breeding season that may otherwise be all too short (from his standpoint). But a lonesome stallion will all too easily become frustrated, rank, and difficult to handle.

When designing your stabling and pasturing plans, then, it helps to try to keep your stallion's needs in mind. Remember that it's written in his nature to be the herd boss, alert to every movement around "his" farm, people, and mares. If he is to have a shed and pasture arrangement that allows him to come and go at will (by far the happiest arrangement for him), try to make it central to the farm's activities so he can oversee them. If his mares are in sight most of the time, and if people have to pass him a million times a day in the course of normal activity (thus necessitating a simple greeting or a pat), he'll be a much happier and better socialized pony than he will be if you cloister him away in a special stallion barn, stall, or paddock tucked away where he has no access to social life. If it isn't possible to keep him turned out with all of your other ponies, it might be possible to turn him out with a bred mare (preferably a sensible, no-nonsense kind of girl who will neither bully him nor put up with unasked-for advances) so that he'll have the company he craves.

Chapter

9

THE HEALTHY PONY

It's easy to understand why breeders these days feel that their ponies are becoming nothing better than equine pin cushions. Many of us remember an era when a routine vaccination against EEE, WEE, and Tetanus were all that were recommended by our vets every year, added to a biannual deworming administered via stomach tube. The diseases have certainly always existed. But it used to be that when horses and ponies contracted them, it was a matter of quarantining the individuals or the farm, treating them as best as possible, burning the bodies and residues, praying for good luck, or taking the losses.

We now have vaccines that provide protection against numerous conditions that formerly threatened to wipe out entire breeding herds or foal crops. The need to use them has become more important due to the rising percentage of horses and ponies that now live in the crowded quarters of boarding stables, and the wide range of travel undertaken by even the most casual trail rider in search of company, competition, and new scenery. These combine to bring animals in contact with each other (and each other's regional diseases) with a frequency and intensity that was formerly unknown. The effect is that contagious viruses and bacterial infections are spread more easily than ever before, while containing and treating them to prevent their spread is more difficult.

Vaccinating your ponies is quite literally the cheapest insurance you can buy. The vital role this plays in herd health has made itself all too clear recently through frightening stories about the rising number of horses and ponies in some areas of the United States dying from equine encephalomyelitis because their owners were feeling strapped by a bad economy and decided to skip the inoculations for a year. The vaccine is so cheap and so effective when compared to the cost of treatment or the eventual loss of valuable breeding stock that doing without it (and others like it) seems almost a criminal oversight.

Vaccines work by introducing a small amount of killed or inactive virus into a pony's system. On receiving its first inoculation, the pony's system reacts by mounting an antibody reaction to what it perceives as invasion by that disease, which raises its antibody titers. A subsequent booster (required by most vaccines a few weeks following the first inoculation) causes the system to react even more strongly, and it is this second response that raises antibody titers to their most effective and long-lasting levels. Thereafter, the pony usually only requires an annual booster to maintain an effective level of resistance to the condition in question. This can vary, of course. Your vet will be able to help you in deciding what will be the optimum type and frequency of vaccinations in your region.

The following list of diseases and conditions contains only the most commonly vaccinated against in most areas. It cannot be stressed too highly that all breeders, no matter how large, small, educated, or experienced, should discuss individual needs thoroughly with a qualified vet and become educated as to the particular requirements of specific locations, climates, and situations. Additional information on reportable diseases and the need to protect against them can be easily obtained by calling your state veterinarian. You have a huge investment in your breeding stock. It would be foolhardy to risk losing it through illness, sterility, or death caused by any one of the number of preventable viruses and bacterial infections that can rip through a barn and ruin a breeding program in a startlingly short period of days.

Eastern and Western encephalomyelitis (EEE and WEE) (Sleeping Sickness) are strains of a disease spread by mosquitoes.

It is always fatal. Vaccination against both forms, given in a single dose, is a highly effective deterrent. In some areas, you may also need protection against the Venezuelan form of EE, and the prevalence and growth of EEE and WEE in many parts of the United States in recent years has caused some vets in high-risk areas to strongly recommend vaccination more than once a year.

Tetanus spores are always present in the environment, and ponies are extremely susceptible to contracting it if they aren't protected against it. Again, this condition is usually fatal, although affected animals can be saved *if* treatment with tetanus antitoxin administered intravenously is begun *early* enough. An annual vaccination is a must to ensure your ponies' safety. The tetanus vaccine is widely available in a three-way dose that includes EEE and WEE, as well as a four-way dose that adds flu.

Rabies is endemic (always present in a certain portion of a population) to raccoons, skunks, foxes, and other small animals. Bats can also carry a form of it. Once contracted, the disease is always fatal, but the rabies vaccine is one of the most successful ever established in providing a barrier of protection against a fatal condition. In recent years, it has become more and more clear that horses and ponies, as well as dogs and cats, *must* be inoculated against the condition annually; not just for the sake of the animals' health, but for the protection of their owners. A pony that contracts rabies may take as long as ten days to show clinical signs of the disease, which does its work by destroying its host's nervous system and is passed on via contact with the saliva of affected animals. Usually this occurs when the ill animal bites one that is healthy, thus providing an opening for the disease to enter. Any open wound or even a scratch that already exists will do. If you consider the amount of time you spend wiping equine saliva off of your hands and clothing, you can see how easily it can be contracted.

Equine influenza and *rhinopneumonitis* are highly contagious respiratory diseases that, while not always fatal, are much less expensive to prevent than they are to treat. Flu (symptomatically similar to our human flu) is frequently picked up in any high-stress situation where groups of ponies congregate at close quarters. The same situations can lead to a high risk of contracting rhino, an equine form of herpesvirus. This occurs in three forms. The first is respiratory, and is a leading cause of upper respiratory illness in young horses. The second has been proven to cause abortion, and is the cause of "abortion storms" that occur when the condition sweeps through an unprotected band of broodmares; devastating to a breeder. The third and rarer neurological form of the disease is a horrific condition that is frequently fatal, always very debilitating, and when contracted requires the strict quarantine of entire barns as well as aggressive treatment that is expensive and not always successful.

New forms of vaccines are constantly being tested for a greater degree of protection against the respiratory and abortogenic forms of Rhino. As yet there is no effective vaccine against the neurological form, although there may be some cross-protection offered by the other two. Some years ago there was a great deal of concern over the use of vaccines using what's known as a "modified live virus," one that is *not* dead and thus capable of causing animals to "shed" the virus so that if once given, it would exist on your farm as a potential problem forever after. "Killed" vaccines that do not have this effect have now existed for some time. Even if your broodmares never leave the farm, they will require protection from flu and rhino exposure brought about by returning performance ponies and outside mares. For their own protection, all stallion owners should insist that every mare arriving on the farm be vaccinated against them.

Postvaccination resistance to the flu and rhino viruses is very short-lived, declining rapidly after two to three months. For this reason, many vets strongly suggest that ponies that are in transit or heavy competition be boostered at regular intervals to maintain a high level of immunity during the busy season. Likewise, bred mares should be given a vaccine specific to the abortogenic strain of rhino in the third, fifth, seventh, and ninth months of pregnancy.

Potomac horse fever, formerly a disease particular to more southerly and low-lying regions of the United States, has been spreading steadily outward from its original locations. PHF causes extreme illness among afflicted animals, with high

SAMPLE VACCINATION SCHEDULE

For Foals:

At birth: Tetanus antitoxin. Vitamin E/selenium if indicated by vet.

At 60–75 days: First vaccination against eastern and western forms of encephalitis (and/or Venezuelan, as indicated by vet), tetanus, flu, and rhinopneumonitis. These can be given on two separate days: EWT on one, flu and rhino on another, to minimize risk of reactions.

After 3 months: Potomac horse fever and rabies.

Note: Booster all vaccinations except rabies three to four weeks after the initial dose to raise antibody titers to effective levels.

For Broodmares:

Vaccinate against the abortogenic form of rhinopneumonitis in the third, fifth, seventh, and ninth months of pregnancy. Regular supplementation with vitamin E and selenium, if indicated by your vet.

Vaccinate against eastern and western (and/or Venezuelan, as above) forms of encephalitis; tetanus, rabies, and flu (administered in one four-way injection) one month before expected foaling date to ensure the highest possible antibody titers. This high immunity will be passed to the foal in a process called "passive transfer" through the mare's colostrum, which provides the foal's only early defense against infection.

For Mature Ponies:

Early spring: Vaccinate early in the season against EWT (as above), flu/rhino, rabies, Potomac horse fever (where indicated), and strangles (where and if indicated). In some situations, vaccination against equine viral arteritis may be necessary. Your vet will advise you about this and other vaccinations that are specific to your region or the exposure of your ponies to numbers of other animals during competition, travel, or other high-risk situations.

Additional protection against flu/rhino: May be indicated as often as every two months in ponies that are in heavy work and in frequent contact with other animals off-farm.

Additional protection against the eastern, western and Venezuelan forms of encephalitis: May be indicated in certain regions of the country, requiring a second autumn vaccination to maintain high immunity.

fever, violent (or "firehose") diarrhea, and subsequent critical dehydration, frequently leading to death. While no vaccines have yet been discovered to be 100 percent effective in preventing the disease entirely, they have been proven to be *at least* 80 percent effective as a barrier against contracting it at all. In instances when vaccinated horses and ponies do get it, they are likely to be far less ill and have a far better recovery rate than unprotected animals. Immunity lasts for six months. This is another inoculation that is strongly recommended among ponies that are likely to come into contact with those from areas where the disease is prevalent.

Strangles is another condition contracted in high-risk, high-stress situations such as heavy campaigning, extensive trucking from place to place, and crowded conditions. A bacterial infection, it is spread via an arthropod vector rather than directly from pony to pony, affecting the upper respiratory tract and the lymph nodes, primarily of the head. It tends to be more common in younger horses and ponies. Although it's a disgusting disease to deal with, and requires extreme care to avoid its spread, the mortality rate is very low. Once recovered, a pony retains immunity for six months. Vaccination twice yearly is thus frequently recommended in warm climates.

Many vets have mixed feelings about vaccinating against strangles unless conditions demand it. One reason is that the vaccine's side effect is the possible contraction of a very dangerous condition known as *Purpura Hemoragica*, which is far more life threatening and more difficult to treat than strangles itself. Another is simply that vaccination against bacterial infections is not as effective as those against viral conditions. When in doubt, discuss the pros and cons of this inoculation with your vet, who will be able to advise you in light of your ponies' specific situations.

There is no known cure as yet for *equine infectious anemia* (EIA or swamp fever), a disease that is spread among equine populations via blood (something it bears in common with the AIDS virus) by horseflies, mosquitoes, and other bloodsucking insects whose original hosts were certain birds native to swampy areas. By extension, it can certainly also be spread by tainted needles. EIA has been the subject of hot debate for many years. The only test for the disease remains the Coggins (or A.G.I.D.) test, which detects the presence of an immune response to the disease in an animal's system. *This is possibly the only situation in which an immune response to a disease is bad rather than good.* In some parts of the country animals that test positive are still subject to euthanasia or a life spent in a completely screened and isolated stall. There is no vaccine to protect against the disease, and its eradication from the population is the only known control.

It is an undeniably drastic method, however, especially to those who lose valued friends, performers, and breeding stock. This has caused many people to insist that the test is meaningless, and that positive horses and ponies pose no threat to a general population. The truth is a little more complex. While it's certainly correct that some horses and ponies are indeed immune and may never pass the disease on, it's equally possible that others may be vectors for it without ever being symptomatic themselves. EIA is dangerous enough that until the time comes when an effective vaccine has been developed, a breeder's safest course is to honor the need for a negative Coggins test annually on all ponies, to demand them from all incoming stock, and to avoid any situation in which they are not mandatory.

DEWORMING

Internal parasites are an omnipresent fact of a pony's existence. Most adult ponies develop a certain tolerance to their presence in their systems. Nevertheless, the modern need to keep animals in more crowded and less changeable quarters provides conditions that encourage more frequent reinfestation and subsequent overload that a free-roaming herd would not be exposed to. Most pony owners today are aware of the dangers of internal parasites in terms of general unthriftiness, poor health, and even bouts of colic that can range from mild to fatal. But *why* do parasites cause this kind of problem, and why is the much-vaunted rotational deworming program so essential to preventing them? A brief description of the life and times of your ponies' four most persistent parasitic enemies—strongyles (large and small), ascarids, tapeworms, and bots—may help to answer these critical questions.

Strongyles (also known as bloodworms) are the most potentially lethal parasites to adult ponies, and also the ones most difficult to eliminate. They quickly build up resistance to most anthelmintics (dewormers), and are tolerant of a broad range of natural conditions. Their life cycle begins when eggs laid in the pony's intestine are passed on to pastures, paddocks, and stalls via your pony's manure. When temperature and humidity are optimum (anywhere from 45 degrees to 100 degrees Fahrenheit), the eggs hatch and fairly quickly go through the first two of five larval stages.

Large strongyles become infective in stage three. Ingested by the pony as it grazes or cleans hay off the floor of a stall, they migrate to the large intestine, attach themselves to a part of the intestinal wall known as the submucosa, and begin to feed. In their fourth larval stage, they migrate further into the small arteries that provide blood to the entire intestinal tract and hindlegs, robbing these organs of vital nutrients. In heavy infestations they can damage the arteries so badly that the blood supply is lost entirely, and in extreme cases they can rupture the artery itself. In stage five they migrate back to the gut, where adults lay eggs, beginning a new cycle.

Small strongyles differ from the large in that they don't migrate as much. After ingestion in the third larval stage they attach themselves to the lining of the cecum and large colon, where they live out most of their nasty little lives essentially poking holes in these organs and robbing the blood of the nourishment essential to their healthful functioning. In large numbers they can cause permanent damage to the organs, leading to colic and death.

Prolonged freezing and thawing cycles can kill strongyle eggs, but in moderate temperatures they can survive for up to two years before hatching or dying. Eggs laid in the autumn that make it to the third stage of larval development before freezing temperatures occur can last for as long as five months, do not die when frozen, and are in fact protected by cold temperatures and snow.

Ascarids (or roundworms) are most dangerous in young ponies, which have not developed any resistance to them, but are somewhat easier to control in mature ponies if early damage has been prevented. Ascarids have four larval stages. In this case, eggs are ingested while grazing, and the larvae hatch in the intestine before migrating to the liver, where they live and feed until reaching the infective second stage. At this point they migrate to the lungs, are coughed up the bronchial tree, swallowed, and resettled in the center (or lumen) of the small intestine. Here, they compete with their host directly for the nutrients present in feed, thus robbing your ponies of all the good grain, hay, and supplements you thought you were giving them.

A mass kill of ascarids can be extremely dangerous to a heavily infested pony, causing impaction (clogging) and even rupture of the small intestine. Far better to treat them aggressively from the start to prevent this from occurring.

Tapeworms were not recognized as a problem in horses until relatively recently, but they are both extremely difficult to kill (the only anthelmintic that affects them is pyrantel pamoate in a double dose), and if killed in a mass in a heavily infested pony can cause either impaction or a condition called "intussusception," in which one part of the intestine actually telescopes into another part. Both of these agonizing and often fatal conditions can be caused when tapeworms settle in an opening about the diameter of a golf ball that unites the small and large intestines, thus restricting the flow of material through that opening into the large intestine during the digestive process.

Tapeworm ranges in frequency and perniciousness from region to region. Most have now reported it, and some ponies are more susceptible to it than others. It's best to assume that it's a potential problem and treat for it once a year in accordance with your vet's recommendation.

Nearly every horse and pony owner is familiar with *bots*, those flies that lay their eggs on the hair of a pony's legs, neck, stomach, flanks, etc. The eggs are ingested when ponies scratch these areas. The eggs then travel to the stomach, where they hatch. Once hatched, bot larvae attach themselves to the lining of the stomach and intestine, where they suck blood and rob their

CLASSES OF ANTHELMINTICS AND COMMONLY USED PASTE DEWORMERS

Class 1. Tetrahydropyrimidine (pyrantel pamoate)
> Used in: Strongid-P, Strongid-T, and Strongid-C

Class 2. Benzimidazoles
> Used in: Athelcide EQ
>> Rintal
>> Benzelmin
>> Panacur (recommended safe for use in foals)
>> Telmin
>> Cutter

Class 3: Ivermectin
> Used in: Eqvalan
>> Zimectrin

Dewormers containing Trichlorfon (an organo phosphate) are additionally used in autumn for the control of bots. Trichlorfon is frequently used in conjunction with a benzimidazole in one product such as Benzelmin Plus. Ivermectin is also effective against bots. No other classes of wormer are.

Strongid is recommended for the control of tapeworm. The recommended treatment is a double dose administered once a year. No other class of dewormer (and no lesser amount of Strongid) is effective against this parasite.

hosts of vital nutrients. In the final stage, larvae are passed out of the system in manure, where adult flies continue the cycle. In severe cases, bots can cause colic and even the rupture of intestinal linings, leading to death of the host pony.

Bots are more easily controlled than some other parasites, in that a diligent owner can make a severe dent in the egg population simply by scraping them off of a pony's body as soon as they're seen. Deworming once a year after hard frost with Trichlorfon is also effective, but some vets do not like it because of its tendency to make certain animals colicky. Ivermectin is an

RECOMMENDED DEWORMING ROTATION

Adult ponies: Deworm every two months alternating products containing each class of anthelmintic. For example, April: ivermectin; June: pyrantel pamoate; August: ivermectin; October: benzimidazole, etc. Once a year, use a double dose of pyrantel pamoate to control tapeworm.

Note: Broodmares should not be dewormed in the first and last stages of pregnancy. *When deworming, do not use products containing organo phosphates.* They aren't safe for bred mares. Some vets recommend using only ivermectin for broodmares.

Foals: Deworm once a month for the first twelve months, using the same rotation as above. After twelve months, go on regular farm rotation. Products with a high safety rating for youngstock and a high efficacy in control of ascarids are recommended. Read labels or consult with your vet for specific products fulfilling these criteria.

Note: A twice-yearly fecal egg count is strongly recommended to monitor parasite control on your farm. In certain cases, your vet may recommend a different rotation or different timing, depending upon your individual situation.

effective means of breaking the cycle by ridding the pony of its internal larval load.

The toughness and durability of these and other parasites, their ability to adapt to different climates, environments, and anthelmintic groups, and the dangers of allowing a heavy infestation of any of them to occur makes it easy to understand why an aggressive approach to their control is so vital. Most veterinarians now recommend deworming programs that range from every six weeks to every two months, using a rotating roster of dewormers.

By rotation, your vet means using different *classes* of anthelmintics each time you deworm your ponies, rather than simply different *brand names*. This can get a little confusing. Say, for instance, that you have given your ponies a dose of Rintal paste, and for your next rotation you decide to switch to Anthelcide-EQ instead. You think you've changed dewormers, but in fact you haven't. A closer look at the *class* of anthelmintic contained in these products will tell you that the former uses febantel and the latter uses oxibendazole, both benzimidazole derivatives. Benzimidazoles are the largest class of dewormers on the market, and also unfortunately the ones to which parasites have developed the most resistance. This is not to say that they aren't useful in a rotational program; they are. But they aren't any good at all if they're all you use.

To be truly rotational, your deworming schedule must also incorporate products containing tetrahydropyrimidine (pyrantel pamoate, and the only class effective against tapeworm) and, of course, ivermectin. Ivermectin operates differently than other anthelmintics, acting by paralyzing parasites rather than poisoning them outright, so that they essentially starve to death. In a heavily infested pony, this can be beneficial when beginning a deworming program by preventing a sudden mass die-off of the kind that can result from an aggressive deworming with another product. It has also been found effective against forms of parasites that haven't previously been touched by other traditional anthelmintics. Even so, it should *not* be considered a panacea. Overuse of any product risks resistance to it being developed by the parasite it's meant to control.

Your vet will be happy to help you develop a deworming program that will be tailored to your specific needs. One good way to help him or her to focus on these is to have a fecal exam done on your ponies once or twice a year. All this requires is that you put a very small amount of manure from a fresh pile into a plastic sandwich bag, label it, and take it by your clinic. The overall cost will be about the same as one dose of dewormer, and it may end up saving you a considerable amount of time and money over the course of a year.

Besides a good deworming rotation, consistent pasture management is essential to the control of internal parasites. Regular removal of manure from paddocks as well as stalls is a great first step in ensuring that your ponies don't immediately re-infect themselves. Manure should *not* be spread on pastures that are in current use or about to be used; the eggs present will simply be ingested as soon as your ponies have been dewormed, thus beginning the cycle all over again.

In addition, large pastures should be rotated, dragged, and rested as frequently and for as many months as possible to expose eggs and larvae to light, heat, and freeze/thaw cycles, depending on the season. Your vet and your county extension service can advise you on an effective system of pasture rest and rotation for your region as well as for your individual requirements. In general, at least a three-month rest of your pastures can be very beneficial in easing the parasite load.

YOUR FRIEND, THE FARRIER

The secret to a sound pony is its feet. If these are not cared for properly, the rest will certainly suffer. Even if your ponies go barefoot all year, they will require routine care from a good farrier to maintain good hoof health and proper growth. Ponies have notoriously hard feet, and they can get very long before breaking or chipping. This leads to a great deal of strain being put on pasterns, fetlocks, and their supporting tissues, and a broken off

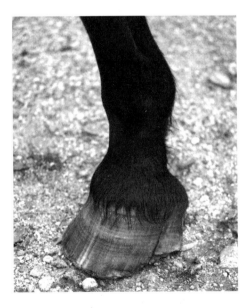

Even the best feet will suffer badly if not tended to regularly by a farrier.

155

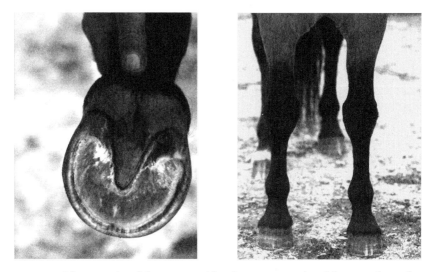

A pony with exceptional feet may, with adequate care, be able to perform for years without shoes in some situations. This pony's feet typify much that is best in native breeds in size, shape, and durability.

foot is an invitation to lameness and unevenness. In addition, youngstock require regular attention to their feet to ensure that no limb deformities are created by those that have been allowed to grow, break, and chip themselves into abnormalities that will be difficult if not impossible to correct later on.

Setting up a regular trimming schedule is yet another way that you will save money in the long run. Even if your ponies' needs vary from one individual and one season to the next, a regular schedule encourages the discovery of minor problems such as cracks, splits, or chips, so that they can be dealt with before they become major headaches. It also enables the farrier to become familiar with each of your ponies so that he or she will know when something is just slightly different than before, or whether there's an inkling that a problem may be developing that neither of you had noticed yet.

A trim every eight weeks for idle ponies is often sufficient to keep problems from developing. If any of your ponies are shod, you'll need to have shoes reset and feet evened off every six to eight weeks. A pony with cracks, bruises, or other injuries will require more frequent attention until the foot has been returned to soundness.

Ponies that are shod through the competitive season benefit greatly from having their shoes pulled during the "down" part of the year. Leaving them barefoot to let nail holes grow out, to provide good ground-to-frog contact and foot expansion, in addition to stimulating healthy horn growth, will help your ponies stay sound and healthy for many years to come.

Chapter

10

MAKING SURE THAT
ONE PLUS ONE EQUALS THREE

What follows can only be a general practical discussion on the process of breeding ponies. All serious breeders should take every opportunity to attend the breeding symposiums offered annually by most equine clinics throughout the United States and Canada, and make use of the many excellent books available on breeding that go into far more detail than is possible here.

There are three basic methods of covering mares: pasture breeding, where mares and stallions live together and mate on their own schedule; hand breeding, where stallion and mare are presented to one another while under the control of handlers; or breeding via artificial insemination using either fresh or frozen semen. Each method has its uses, which will of course vary according to need and setup.

PASTURE BREEDING

Pasture (or "natural") breeding has largely fallen out of favor in this era of technology, control, timing, sanitation, and convenience, but there is still a lot to be said for it. Stallions that can be turned out with their mares are generally much happier than

Stallions are usually happiest if they can be turned out with a favored mare. Here, the Connemaras Aladdin (Erin Laddie x Fox Ridge Irish Lady) and Far Above's Katherine (Far Above's Shannon x *Lambay Maeve) wait politely for their supper. *Photo: Catherine Mack.*

those that have no contact with them except during the acts of teasing and breeding. Mares that are bred naturally also tend to have a greater chance of settling than those that are bred on a human timetable, in spite of the diagnostic tools we have at our disposal to predict the approximate moment of ovulation and the optimum time to breed.

Although the average mare comes into heat for approximately five days every twenty-one days, some will have cycles that are longer, and some will be shorter. Some will ovulate off of a smaller follicle, some off a larger one. Some mares will stand only on the day they ovulate. Others will stand for days on end. Some mares with reproductive difficulties may produce what looks like a breedable follicle, only to reabsorb it before it ripens. Almost every stallion owner has at one time or another had to deal with an irate owner who sent a mare to the farm with a follicle "that should be good on Tuesday," only to be greeted with the information that neither the mare nor the stallion agreed. Catching these mares on the rare occasions that they actually do ovulate can be a case of rare psychic luck—or of a pasture breeding situation in which the mare and stallion are free to get together at that one brief moment in time when everything's right. In taking a good deal of human guesswork out of the equation, pasture breeding can alleviate the cost of constant veterinary intervention to check the state of a mare's follicular activity, and the reordering of daily life to revolve around the possibility that a certain mare may or may not need to be covered on a particular day.

There is a downside, of course. In pasture breeding, there is always the possibility of injury to both mare and stallion if the wrong individual gets the wrong idea at the wrong time. Stallions frustrated with a mare's behavior can land a laming kick or a damaging chomp on what may be an extremely valuable show mare's hide. Stallions, likewise, are extremely vulnerable to a crippling kick to the head or to the genitals. These things do happen often enough for them to be a legitimate concern. And in any situation that involves a group of mares turned out with a stallion, there are bound to be petty jealousies that erupt into kicking fights, even among mares that are usually tractable. Some old broodmares become so possessive of "their" stallion that they can actually keep him from covering other mares that are in heat.

People are also frequently concerned about the sanitary aspects of pasture breeding. In a closed system—a group of mares and a stallion that are turned out exclusively with one another all year without being exposed to other breeding ponies—this is not a large worry. As long as both your stallion and your mares are free of infection and kept in good health on clean pasture with adequate attention paid to keeping their genital areas moderately clean, you should be fine. After all, ponies have been breeding successfully in the wild for thousands of years without benefit of any human control of their relative cleanliness. In some sense, we can even assume that natural selection would favor breeding stock in the wild that was resistant to infection, easy to breed and settle, and that did not make a habit of killing or crippling each other in the process. Any situation that is crowded, dirty, or has a high number of unknown outside mares moving in and out of the established group throughout the breeding season, however, can certainly raise the danger and incidence of infections being spread among an entire group.

HAND BREEDING

While more labor intensive for the owner and handlers, hand breeding is still reasonably natural, and (theoretically, anyway) comes with the added assurance of control that minimizes any exposure to injury or infection while maximizing the possibility of getting a mare in foal by the simple fact of knowing exactly how many times she's been successfully covered by the stallion during her heat cycle.

"Hand breeding" as a phrase actually covers a lot of ground. At its most elaborate, it can involve a covered breeding shed with rubber matted floors, an attached lab, and assorted technicians and handlers in white coats. One technical manual suggests five: one to hold the mare's head, one to tie a foreleg up, one to hold her tail out of the way, one on the stallion's head, and another to help him enter the mare, hold a breeding roll (a sort of a bolster held under the mare's tail that prevents a large stallion from penetrating too deeply and injuring the mare's vagina) in place, and collect some of the semen that invariably spills out of the vagina when the stallion dismounts. That semen is then taken to the lab next door to have it looked at immediately on a warmed slide under a warm microscope to check for sperm count and motility. On the other end of the spectrum is the rather elderly breeder I once met who tied his mare with her face to the barn wall (using three ropes, no less), brought out his stallion on about ten feet of fraying leadrope, and stood as far away as possible. In between these two illustrations are the methods used by most small breeders, which rely on two people, a well-behaved mare and stallion, accurate observation, and adequate teasing.

Teasing (which can be thought of as equine foreplay) is an essential part of breeding, and especially important in hand

Pasture breeding can be a successful option if you're very sure of the good disposition and herd manners of your mares and stallion.

breeding. First, it's the best natural indicator of a mare's willingness to be covered. In addition, it gives nervous maiden mares that haven't been exposed to stallions a little time to become acclimated to the idea of being chatted up by this noisy, demanding, and boisterous animal in relative safety.

There are various ways to tease mares, any of which may prove useful in different situations. One nice way to start is to have mares that are to be bred in a paddock next to the stallion's, separated by an alleyway wide enough to keep them from touching noses across it. The stallion will "talk" to the mares periodically throughout the day (and night), and generally those mares that are coming into heat will respond by coming to the fence with tails raised, looking interested in his advances. Those who aren't will either ignore him entirely or rush the fence with ears pinned and tails swishing, threatening to knock his head off if he doesn't mind his own business.

Mares that are showing signs of estrus can be led to the door of the stallion's stall to touch noses, smell, chat, and so on, or the stallion can be brought to the mare's stall door. Some breeders build a separate solid standing partition or teasing bar some distance from the barn to allow safe interaction in the inevitable process of squealing, striking, and kicking. This system has the benefit of separating "teasing" and "stall" in the stallion's mind, so that he doesn't think that he's about to breed a mare every time he walks by the barn.

During teasing, the handlers involved must pay strict attention to the whereabouts of their charges' feet at all times, staying on the left side about even with the shoulder but standing away several feet so as not to risk being accidentally struck or stepped on. They must be prepared to pull stallion or mare away from the teasing bar immediately if they show any tendency to whirl and kick or to rear and strike. If the mare reacts in an aggressive manner and shows none of the usual signs of estrus ("winking" vulva, wide hind-legged stance, raised tail, squatting and urinating, and the obvious willingness to stand like a rock), the teasing session must be ended *immediately*. Most pony stallions are tractable enough to tease the mares they breed, unlike the stallions on many large horse farms that are used for breeding only, with a special teaser (frequently a pony) used to do the frustrating part of the job. But even the best-mannered pony stallion is bound to get pretty excited and demanding during this necessary process. The handler must thus walk the fine line between demanding good manners and allowing the stallion to do his job. A part of this is learning to recognize within moments when a mare is not in heat so that the stallion's frustration and the mare's aggressiveness are not allowed to escalate.

In preparation for covering, attention to basic cleanliness of mare and stallion is important. The mare's vulva and surrounding area should be washed with mild soap and warm water (don't overdo the soap, it can be spermicidal) and rinsed, and her tail wrapped for at least the length of the dock so that it won't be in the way. The stallion's penis should likewise be washed and rinsed as quickly and deftly as possible. Both stallion and mare should wear sturdy halters with the chain of a shank run safely over the nose in case extra control is needed. It's very rare that twitches, hobbles, or a strapped up foreleg are necessary. In general, if the whole experience is presented from the start in a manner that is relaxed and matter-of-fact, the mare should respond willingly. Maiden mares may need extra teasing and extra time taken during their first breeding experience. *It's worth the effort.* A good first experience leads to a mare that will be easy to breed forever after.

The breeding location should be open and free from any potentially hazardous obstructions. A large paddock is fine. The mare should stand in the center, with her handler at her head but standing slightly to the left (as you're facing her) to be out of the way of her forelegs, as well as the stallion and his handler. For added safety, both handlers can wear hard hats.

The stallion should approach the mare from the left side, *not* directly from the rear, which may incite a well-placed kick. Again, as in teasing, his handler must stand to the stallion's left with enough contact on the shank to pull him away if needed, but not so much that the pony is restricted. Stallions vary greatly in their breeding behavior. Some like to mount immediately, others like to engage in some preliminary licking, rubbing, and chat. Don't hurry your stallion; just keep him on the left side, stay clear of his feet and the mare's, keep the shank from being tangled, and be prepared for him to mount so that you don't inadvertently pull him off or get caught by a flying hoof.

When the stallion has mounted and ejaculated, he can be allowed a few seconds before dismounting *if the mare is content to stand*. If she shows any sign of a humped rear or a parting kick, the handler must walk her forward out from under the stallion *immediately*, turning her head to the left so that her hindquarters swing right, out of kicking range of the stallion and his handler.

How often a mare is covered has a great deal to do with how busy a stallion is, whether the mare is being palpated by a vet to determine the presence of a ripe follicle (thus providing a more accurate picture of when she's due to ovulate and an optimum time to cover her), and the stallion's fertility. Sperm can live for up to seventy-two hours in the environment of a mare's reproductive tract, so that *theoretically* a mare could be bred only once in the middle of a heat cycle and be gotten in foal. Most breeders—especially those who are servicing mares with as little veterinary intervention as possible—prefer not to take this risk, and have schedules that may range from breeding every other day, to

THE SAFE APPROACH TO HAND BREEDING

Mare (A) stands in an open area with handler (B) facing her and slightly to the left (her right) side. Stallion (C) approaches from the left side (Arrow D), with handler (E) to his left and slightly away from him, carrying enough slack in the line to allow the stallion to maneuver into breeding position comfortably (F). The stallion handler can move closer if the stallion requires help in entering the mare, but otherwise should be as passive as possible.

the second and forth days, to the third and fifth, to the middle three, or any combination thereof. Researching the success rates of other breeders and their methods, and reading up on the most recent findings of a good equine research clinic can guide you in a schedule that will work on your farm.

ARTIFICIAL INSEMINATION (AI)

The process of collecting semen for shipment to the expectant owner of a mare on the verge of ovulating is something like an exercise in high school chemistry. The stallion is brought to a mare in estrus, as in any ordinary hand breeding situation. The difference here is that you require a third person, who is armed with what's called an artificial vagina (AV), a long cylindrical affair with a heavy latex liner filled with water warmed to approximately thirty-seven degrees Centigrade. Stallions can be very picky about the temperature range they'll accept, so this may vary by a few degrees. An inner liner of either latex or thin plastic is then inserted into the AV and well lubricated with sterile, nonspermicidal jelly. When the stallion mounts a "jump" mare or breeding dummy, the holder of the AV deflects the stallion's penis into it, holding the cylinder at an angle that will allow the ejaculate to drain down the sleeve, through a strainer that separates "gel" from sperm-containing semen, and into a cup or pouch on the end of the sleeve.

This pouch is then separated quickly from the rest of the AV apparatus, and (protected from light, heat, or cold) rushed to the lab, kitchen, or bathroom where there awaits extender, nonspermicidal plastic syringes, and antibiotics, all prewarmed to 37 degrees Celsius. The extender is a mixture that provides the sperm with both food and protection for its journey through the mail before it reaches its destination. It can be readily bought premixed, or you can try making your own using a recipe recommended by your area's equine clinic. Vets vary in their recommendation for the ideal ratio of extender to semen, and a lot depends on the quantity and motility of a stallion's sperm, the length of time in the container, and the highly individual ability of sperm to

166

live through the process of being collected, extended, and shipped. The average is usually about two-to-three parts extender to one part semen. This is carefully measured into another pre-warmed bag (baby bottle liners work well) and gently swirled until well mixed. To this whole witches' brew is added a small amount of antibiotic such as reagent-grade Gentocin or Ticarcillin. Then the whole thing is closed securely, put inside yet another bag, stashed gently in a cup with added ballast material tucked around it so that the whole cup contains a total of 120 cubic centimeters of material, and packed into a shipping container.

These containers are sophisticated units specifically de-signed to provide maximum protection to their fragile contents. They also create an environment that will cool the semen at a specified rate that will hold it in suspension and allow it to arrive at its destination in good shape. They generally consist of a molded plastic exterior roughly the size of a joint compound bucket or a large tub of your favorite feed supplement, and are about 80 percent foam insulation material. Into this casing, two frozen canisters are settled. On top of these, in another Styrofoam-insulated container, sits the cup within which the bagged semen and ballast pouches rest.

The whole process of collecting, preparing, and packaging should take no more than ten minutes, if the semen is to remain viable. The packed unit is then shipped via the quickest route possible to the owner. The chemistry project continues when the container and its contents reach its destination. Here vet and mare owner meet to wrap the mare's tail, wash her genital area carefully, unpack the semen, draw it up with another sterile non-spermicidal syringe, attach this to a sterile infusion pipette, and inject the extended semen into the uterus, where it will regain warmth, life, and motility in the mare's reproductive tract.

Breeding artificially is an option whose use has exploded exponentially in the last few years. Improved shipping methods, better storage media, and a more educated base of practitioners have all combined to increase its effectiveness. Its usefulness as a tool has been proven repeatedly. In the case of breeds that are still fairly rare, breeding via transported semen vastly increases the breeder's ability to find and use stallions that will be the best matches for their mares without having to settle for one that's closer to home. Some mares that don't travel well will settle more easily when bred at home. In some cases the cost of shipping semen is far less than that of shipping and boarding a mare that may already have a foal at foot.

On the other hand, it can also be more expensive, more of a hassle, and less convenient than simply sending a mare away to be bred. For mare owners, there can be sizable vet bills incurred during the daily monitoring of follicular activity before the actual shipment of and insemination with the transported semen. If your mare looks like she's going to ovulate on a day when the stallion owner doesn't ship, you run the risk of missing that heat period entirely. And if she ovulates on Sunday, you're looking at extra vet charges as well as the ability of your carrier to deliver on that day. Sometimes semen that has been extended, packed, or handled poorly can be dead when it arrives. Sometimes the mare ovulates off a smaller follicle than expected and the insemination takes place one vital day too late.

Stallion owners have their share of problems, too. Most have received calls early in the morning one fine April day from a mare owner requesting that semen be shipped *that day*, even though no prior warning had been given. This may not be a problem for large and well-equipped breeding farms that specialize almost exclusively in transported semen and that keep certain mares in heat year-round to jump from. Nor may it trouble those that keep a supply of frozen urine from mares in estrus to be smeared on a special breeding mount (or phantom) that a stallion has been trained to accept in lieu of a live mare. But small breeders who don't use phantoms and who rely on having another mare in heat are limited to shipping semen only when they have a mare in heat that can be used as a jump from which to collect. Many don't have immediate access to vets or nearby labs and clinics whose facilities are available at the drop of a hat, or staff on hand who do nothing but collect and ship while the owner is off competing or buying the week's grain.

Ensuring the success of breeding artificially thus demands a high level of communication between all parties. The mare owner must be intimately acquainted with the length of the mare's cycles and the next optimum time to breed her, notifying the stallion owner *well in advance* of this date; preferably during the heat before the one to be bred on. The stallion owner can then be prepared to adjust a few days in either direction, and won't be surprised by sudden and totally unexpected phone calls. If the breeding is going to involve a mare being brought into heat early in order to coincide with another's cycle, some advance agreement must be made as to whose mare it's going to be: the stallion owner's or the mare to be bred. And if the mare owner intends to breed more than one mare to the same stallion, it makes sense to get these mares on the same breeding cycle to make the most efficient use of the whole collection and shipping process. *This does not mean that you'll only owe one booking and stud fee.* Two bred mares still incur two sets of fees, but you will be saving on the shipment and vet costs, which can be considerable.

As the time for collection draws close, mare owner and stallion owner need to be in close contact about pinning down the actual day of shipment. Up to two days before ovulation is optimum; mares inseminated at this time have as great a chance of settling as those bred on the day of ovulation, and a much greater chance than those bred even hours afterward. Most stallion owners will provide mare owners with two separate bags of extended semen so that two inseminations twenty-four hours apart can be administered to optimize the chances of impregnating the mare, but check to make sure that this is standard procedure with the stallion owner concerned.

After the mare has been inseminated, the stallion owner needs his or her container back as quickly as possible for use in the next shipment, and will need to know as soon as possible whether your mare has settled. If she has, it will be reported to the breed society so that your foal will be eligible for registration.

PREPARING YOUR MARES FOR BREEDING

Breeding mares is not cheap, and unfortunately there can never be a *guarantee* that your mare will settle right away. Whether bred by live cover or via transported semen, ponies and horses are not statistically the most fertile of mammals. For healthy maiden mares, a successful breeding rate is considered to be around 80 percent. For mares that have produced foals, the figure can subsequently fall as low as 35 percent, dependent on whether the mare in question ever contracted an infection, how quickly it was cleaned up, whether any damage was done to the uterus, or whether difficult foalings have left too much scar tissue to allow her to maintain a subsequent pregnancy.

Many owners try to keep their cash outlay to a minimum by skimping on things like the length of time a mare is left at the farm, or veterinary intervention of any sort, or even by neglecting to have biopsies performed. *This is never recommended, and it is rarely successful.* The only real way to breed on a shoestring is to be absolutely prepared to do everything necessary to optimize your mare's chances of conception and settling *before* problems arise and you start throwing money away.

To begin with, it's wise to have all stressful procedures taken care of well in advance of your mare being bred, to keep her in a mellow state of mind as well as in the peak of health. She should have all of her routine vaccinations, a negative Coggins, her teeth floated, her feet trimmed, and a recent deworming all attended to a minimum of thirty days before traveling to the farm or being bred at home. It is hoped that you will also have kept track of her heat cycles from the earliest possible part of the season so that you know roughly when to expect her to come into heat.

Several months before the heat on which you expect to breed, a uterine culture should be performed to make absolutely sure that there is no infection present. This can only be done when the mare is in heat and the cervix is open, and consists of a swab being inserted to collect a small amount of material from the lining of the uterus. This will be smeared on a glass slide to be cultured for the presence of any infection. A clean culture will be demanded by any stallion owner before your mare will be allowed on his or her farm, but even if you're breeding with artificial insemination, it's a necessary precaution. The smallest low-grade infection will be enough to keep a mare from conceiving, or can cause her to reabsorb or abort an embryo.

In the case of an older mare that hasn't foaled for a couple of years, it's also wise to have a uterine biopsy performed. This procedure, which relies on actually pinching off a minute piece of the uterine lining for examination, can tell you whether the uterine lining is healthy enough to provide a good environment for maintaining a pregnancy to term.

There are many factors both hormonal and physiological that can hamper a mare's ability to carry a foal to term. Some of these can be remedied (supplementation with progesterone, for example); others can't (too much scarring of the uterus). Some mares produce foals year in and year out while still carrying on with their careers as performers. Others consistently reabsorb their fetuses early on unless allowed a few months of "down time" in which to relax. Still others refuse to accept a stallion's advances if they're nursing a foal, and so will only produce bi-annually. And there are mares that will refuse the stallion of your dreams altogether for some totally obscure equine reason, while doting on another that you find utterly reprehensible. Ponies are, after all, as individual, and as opinionated, as people.

In the long run it will pay you well to learn about all of the possible obstacles in the way of getting a mare to produce healthy offspring, and to take the steps necessary to remove them. Breeding can be an incredibly frustrating experience, but preparedness, forethought, patience, and a certain acceptance of the fact that we are not really in total control of how or if our mares are going to become good producers, will help put the whole process in perspective, as well as increasing your chances of success.

THE BREEDING CONTRACT

If you stand a stallion with a good performance record, nice off-spring, interesting and useful bloodlines, and have advertised him successfully to boot, chances are good you'll attract some outside mares to your farm to be bred to him. This is a blended pleasure. On one hand, stud fees and board checks can help support your

Sample Breeding Contract

(Should be headed with your farm name, address, and phone)

Thanks for your interest in (stallion name). We are looking forward to having (mare name) arrive on (date) and will do our best to return her home safely in foal.

(Stallion's) 19 __ stud fee is (fee), including a nonrefundable booking fee of (fee) due before your mare arrives. Mare care is (fee) per day. We recommend bringing your mare to (the farm) five to seven days before her next expected heat so that she will have time to settle in before breeding, and request that you leave her here until we are able to have her receive ultrasound for pregnancy fourteen days after her last cover date. All bills are payable when you pick your mare up. If for some reason she does not conceive while at (the farm), or if she fails to produce a foal after leaving here in foal, we offer a free return in the following season. (NOTE: The foregoing is for a return guarantee breeding. No guarantee or guaranteed live foal will, of course, differ in wording.)

For our mutual safety, we request that your mare arrive in good health with the following procedures taken care of:

1. Proper vaccination against EEE, WEE, tetanus, flu, rhino, and rabies. (NOTE: list all required in your area or at your farm.)

2. Deworming within thirty days of arrival.

3. A clean uterine culture (possibly n/a for maiden mares). Biopsy recommended in all mares that have not been bred recently or with histories of breeding problems.

4. Hind shoes must be removed; barefoot all around is best if possible.

5. Current negative Coggins. (NOTE: Should specify how current)

Finally, please call to let us know when to expect you.

To be signed by the owner: (Please bring with you when you arrive.)
I have read and agree to the terms of (farm's) breeding contract for (stallion) in (date). I further understand that with all due caution taken, accidents with horses and ponies can and do happen. I agree to hold harmless (farm), its owners, and agents from any such unforeseeable circumstance. (NOTE: The specifics of releases and hold harmless clauses can vary from state to state. Consult with a legal expert when designing yours to ensure that it has the best chance of protecting you.)

Owner:

Date:

farm and your ponies. On the other, outside mares can be more trouble than they're worth and can bring you nothing but headaches. The trick is to try to maximize the former while minimizing the latter, which requires some attention to detail.

Of maximum importance is a good contract. This is not just to protect yourself; it also lays out in detail every piece of information that the mare owner needs to know to get her mare safely in foal. Your contract should begin by specifying what it is you expect of all mares arriving on your farm. Included should be proof of negative Coggins, vaccinations against everything that you require in your area for both health and peace of mind, deworming within thirty days, a clean uterine culture (and biopsy if called for), and all other basic health needs taken care of as outlined above, including the removal of her hind shoes (very important for your stallion's safety) before being allowed to arrive at your farm. *Don't automatically expect that mare owners will know all this.* Especially if they're new to breeding, a contract that is accompanied by a list of requirements and further suggestions will be welcomed rather than resented, as it will instantly lay to rest about 85 percent of the questions and problems that are likely to arise.

You may also suggest a period of time to leave the mare at your farm. Experienced breeders often request, for instance, that mares arrive at least a few days before their next expected heat to give them time to settle in and become acquainted with their surroundings. It's also frequently recommended that people leave their mares long enough after breeding to be checked in foal via ultrasound, in case they need to be rebred. Finally, you may want to enclose another sheet of paper for your own records and edification that include the mare's name, breeding, and registration number, as well as space for her feeding schedule and amounts, turnout habits, personality quirks, and anything else you may need to know about her while she's on your farm. Especially during the busiest part of the summer when mares are coming and going frequently, it's very useful to have something that you can refer to instead of constantly trying to remember whether it was the bay mare or the grey that tries to kill everybody that she's turned out with, or that founders instantly on grass.

The actual contract agreement will outline the booking fee, stud fee, cost of mare care, how veterinary expenses will be billed, and the terms of payment of the stud and board fees. Booking fees are generally due when the breeding contract is signed, and except in extraordinary circumstances they are usually nonrefundable. Some breeders who offer a "live foal guarantee" expect further payment only of board and vet fees before the mare goes home, the outstanding stud fee being due when the resulting foal stands and nurses. Others offer a slightly different "return guarantee," in which all bills are due before the mare leaves the farm having been checked in foal by ultrasound by a vet. If the mare subsequently reabsorbs the fetus, aborts, or loses her foal before it stands and nurses, the owner is then guaranteed a return service to the same stallion either in that season or the next. *It's very important to state clearly the length of time and the number of services the return is good for.*

Another vital part of the contract is a "hold harmless" clause, which limits your liability in case of any unforeseeable accident. These do happen, even on the best-run farms in the world. It sometimes seems venal to be insisting on this sort of thing from people who may often be our friends and fellow breeders, but most people will appreciate your care and thoroughness. A good contract offers the best possible protection for all parties.

Contracts for breeding via transported semen differ somewhat in their terms. Specifically, they lay out very stringent rules as to the use of semen, limiting it solely to the mare or mares that have been contracted and whose booking fees are paid, and destruction of any that is left over. They also require the signatures of vets, breeders, and owners on both the receiving and shipping ends. Most societies that allow the registration of foals that are the result of AI breedings will provide breeders with their own contract forms that state clearly the regulations that must be met for these foals to be registered with their respective breed societies or halfbred registries. These are generally easily obtained from your society's secretary. AI contracts should also specify who is responsible for what charges. Does the shipping fee include all vet charges? Does it include the cost of overnight or same-day delivery service? These things *must* be stated clearly to alleviate any possible confusion. After this, the terms of the contract—whether it's live foal guarantee, return guarantee, or no guarantee at all—will be the same as for live breeding.

SAMPLE MARE RECORD

(Head with farm name, address, and phone)

Mare's Name: **Owner:**   **Phone:**

Reg.#:   **Sire:**   **Dam:**

Last Vax Date: Against:

Last Deworming Date: Product:

Cultured Clean Date: Biopsied?

(NOTE: You may want to know whether the mare is insured and by whom.)

Feeding Instructions (hay and grain):

We turn mares out daily unless you say otherwise. Any stipulations?

Any foibles, habits, etc., we need to be aware of to keep your mare happy and comfortable while she is at (farm name)?

Any breeding/foaling problems that you know of? (Describe, if they exist.)

Any additional thing we need to be aware of?

Teased Dates:

Bred Dates:

A BRIEF FOALING PRIMER

In breeding and foaling, *education is your best tool*. Your use of available resources such as books, symposia, and the experience of other experienced breeders will build your familiarity and comfort with the whole process of foaling and enable you to help your mare rather than getting in the way. It will also give you the knowledge to recognize instantly whether you are looking at a situation that may require veterinary intervention.

The average gestation period for a normal equine pregnancy ranges from 320 to 345 days. Ninety-nine percent of all foalings

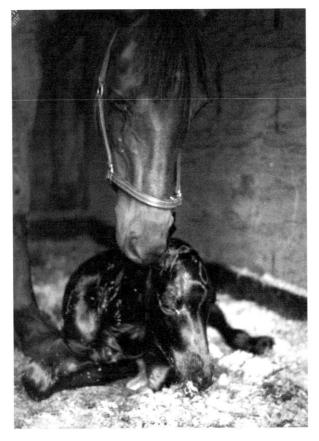

Ninety-nine percent of the time, foaling proceeds in an entirely normal fashion.

176

are perfectly uneventful. But there are some specific things to look for that deserve to be outlined briefly. First, when your mare's water breaks, you should be able to see a front foot, followed by another front foot and a nose, right away. If you don't see anything, or if you see an obvious hindfoot, a forefoot that has no nose or other foot accompanying it, a foot whose sole is facing upward, or a foot protruding from the rectum rather than the vulva, *call your vet immediately*. Any of these signs point to severe malpresentations whose correction is critical to the life of mare and foal alike.

Assuming that none of this is the case, and the foal has slipped out with a minimum of fuss, let the umbilical cord break on its own so that the foal receives all the last-minute nourishment it can through it. Then is the time to get iodine on the navel stump as quickly as possible (before the foal is up and tearing around the stall). Iodine should be reapplied twice in the next twenty-four hours to ensure freedom from infection to this vulnerable area. At this time, the foal should receive an intramuscular dose of tetanus antitoxin. A dose of vitamin E and selenium can also be administered if your vet has recommended it.

Most foals don't need you to dry them or help them to their feet, although in rare instances you may need to go so far as to break the birth sack if it hasn't torn on its own, so that the foal can breathe. Young foals will look very wobbly and disoriented when first staggering around. In the process of looking for the udder they are inclined to try sucking their mothers' forelegs, chests, and even the stall walls. *Try to avoid the impulse to help.* You may actually slow this important process down by getting in the way. If the foal has an obviously strong sucking reflex—you'll be able to tell: Its tongue will be folded up over its upper lip and it will be making sucking noises—and is able to get up again when it inevitably tips over, it's clearly doing fine and will only be confused by well-intentioned intervention. The great majority will have figured out the location and logistics of the meal wagon in three hours' time.

The first milk, or colostrum, is *essential* to the foal's well-being, as it contains *all* the antibodies the foal needs to protect it

A healthy mare and foal—the end product we all aim for. *Photo: Wade Alexander.*

throughout its first several months of life. The passage of these antibodies from mare's colostrum to foal's system is achieved by a process known as passive transfer. *Passive transfer of these critical antibodies will not occur after twenty-four hours*, due to quickly changing cellular structures. If your foal has not nursed within a period of several hours (and if you *know* this to be true from observation throughout that period), call your vet. Some assistance may be required.

Shortly after nursing, your foal will pass the first of the meconium, a dark, sticky substance that has plugged and protected his intestine before birth. He'll strain a bit to get it out, and that's okay. A great deal of straining with no result, however, may indicate constipation. Consult with your vet to see if an enema may be indicated. The passing of the first urine should also be watched, especially in colts. If you see any sign of urine dripping from the umbilicus, call your vet immediately.

Keep an eye on Mama, too. She'll appreciate a bran mash after foaling, and she should be watched to make sure that she passes manure normally. The placenta should be passed within three hours of the foal's birth, checked thoroughly for any tears or fragments that may have been retained, or saved in a bag for the vet to check. Resist the temptation to pull it out when it hangs from the mare's vulva. This can cause it to tear, and result in a piece being left behind in the uterus, a common source of serious infection, foundering, and possible death.

A lot can happen in the critical first twelve hours of life that will bear on the foal's continued health and development. But if all has proceeded smoothly, no veterinary attention may be required until eighteen hours after birth. At this point your vet can give the mare and foal a thorough health check, and a blood sample from the foal will show whether antibody titer levels from the colostrum it received from its dam have achieved optimum levels.

Chapter

11

HANDLING AND TRAINING FOR YOUNGSTOCK AND BROODSTOCK

Foals are born with enormous curiosity and openness to the world, and come equipped with all the instincts they need to grow into adult ponies. Even at a day old they measure and experiment with their place in the world. They nip, they kick, they buck, they taste, they run. They use Mama as a punching bag as often as a source of comfort and nourishment. Mares, like parents, differ in their reaction to this treatment. Some put on a martyred air of long-suffering and tolerate all sorts of painful antics. Others dish out prompt discipline with a sharp nip or butt or a swat with a knee or hock when Junior crosses the line from civilized behavior to rudeness. Be happy if your mare is in the latter category; she will do a lot of the early work of training for you. But your role is still important, because the foal will use you in the same way, and your reactions will dictate its future response to humans throughout its life.

Foals are so impossibly cute that it's easy to laugh at their antics when they buck as we pat them or rear at us in play or chew on us with their little milk teeth. We may remonstrate gently, but fondly reason that there will be plenty of time for discipline later, and convince ourselves that this is temporary behavior that will be outgrown. All too commonly, the end result of this romantic train of thought is an untrammeled yearling that out-weighs its owner by a considerable amount and is capable of doing severe bodily damage to everyone it encounters. All in fun, of course, and never malicious, yet. Professionals cringe at the sight of perfectly rational human beings being towed, bitten, kicked, and generally abused by unruly youngsters that were never taught manners. The common response of the handler to this behavior is a half-hearted tug on the lead with a soft, "Oh, don't do that." Then the lack of attention and respect is excused because "He's never been away from home before" or "That dog (or flag or person or piece of paper or leaf) rattled him." Meanwhile, the formerly cute and fuzzy foal has gotten the idea that he's in charge of the situation. He becomes an equine juve-nile delinquent, pushing his limits with increasing strength and determination until, by the time he's three, he's become very scary and completely unmanageable.

There is no such thing as a moment that's too early to begin handling your foals. Yes, they need time to bond with their dams, and yes, this process can take a couple of days to be firmly cemented. But if you're fortunate or dedicated enough to be pre-sent at the birth, there is no reason in the world why you can't spend a minute helping rub it dry with a towel or simply put your hands all over its body while speaking very gently. This takes a matter of seconds, yet it has been proven repeatedly to be an ade-quate initiation of the foal into the belief that people are both omnipresent and trustworthy. Studies have shown, and breeder experience seconded, that foals handled from birth are more tractable than those that see their first humans hours or days afterward. Certainly all is not lost if your old mare sneaks off into the far corner of your biggest pasture to foal when nobody's look-ing. But try for that initial gentle fondling as soon as possible when she returns—preferably in the close and comforting con-fines of a stall.

It's unfortunate that a foal's first human contact tends to come in conjunction with being stabbed by needles and sloshed with stinging iodine. Try to administer these indignities as quickly and as quietly as possible, preferably before it's steady on its feet. One person can hold it softly with one arm around its chest and another around its haunches. The foal may buck and try to escape, but this is a secure hold on a very young pony that shouldn't be hard for an average-sized person to maintain. It also constitutes an early very simple lesson in submission and trust that can be repeated frequently for short periods over the first few days of life. Foals seem to be born itchy, especially on the top of their tails and the center of their chests, which they can't reach. Couple your hold with a bit of scratching and your foals will quickly learn that being held is not only nonthreatening, it's positively desirable. By the time it's strong enough to be able to break away from you easily (which can be a matter of days), it won't be as inclined to. And foals that grow up feeling that being held by a trusted person is a source of security will often continue to look to their people for comfort when anything new or scary happens to them, which is an added plus throughout their training.

Spend time sitting in the stall with your foals, preferably in a position you can get out of in a hurry if you need to. This means squatting, not sitting cross-legged on the floor. Try talking softly and placing yourself with your hands on your knees, palms up. Foals, like children, come in every permutation of bold to shy, but they are all curious, and they will all approach you if given time and opportunity. A neutral, eye-level position just begs to be investigated. If the foal is very shy, don't force the issue of touching its face, no matter how irresistible those soft muzzles are. You'll make better progress if you start simply by slowly raising a hand to scratch the center of its chest. If it runs off, don't worry—it'll be back. Gradually you'll be able to scratch its chin and then its ears, as well as stroke its legs. This sounds simple to the point of idiocy, but the simplest things are frequently the most effective. Every small move you make now will compound itself tremendously in the future young pony that has been accustomed from day one to being touched and worked with.

As it comes to accept your touch and being held, grooming with a soft brush can teach a foal more about the pleasures of human contact, as well as being a way to further acclimatize it to having all parts of its body, and especially its feet, handled. Again, be quiet about this and go very slowly. Many foals feel trapped if you pick up a foot, and at first a fraction of a second is fine. Build slowly on small successes and you'll have a foal that thinks all this contact is a wonderful game.

Mucking out stalls while mama and baby are in residence is another great training opportunity and a painless way for the foal to get used to the way people move and talk. Move a little more deliberately than normal, and make sure that you keep your muck fork's tines very close to the ground at all times. This is a good chance to assess the relative temperaments of your foals very early on. Shier ones may spend a few days shooting around the stall and keeping Mama between you and them. Bolder ones, conversely, will all but climb into the manure bucket and your lap, and may even insist on tasting the muck fork as it moves from place to place. Time and curiosity will bring the shy ones around, and you'll be better equipped to understand their needs as they get older and serious schooling begins.

The bold ones will probably be the first to need discipline. Tasting everything is normal investigative foal behavior, so they should be allowed to lip at utensils and the like. But if it nips you, you must immediately respond with a quick, sharp swat and a firm *"No!"* Sure, the foal will dash away from you, but if you carry on as if nothing has happened, it'll be soon be back. It *will not* hold your actions against you or be in any way damaged by them. In fact, most foals will try whatever it was that got them into trouble at least once more to see if you really mean it. Make sure you do. Repeat the swat as firmly and as often as necessary to get the point across.

The foal that bucks, rears, and kicks also needs a firm slap and a definitive *"No!"* This is critical, even at the tender age of two days. Twenty-four hours after birth, a foal can do a lot of damage if it clips you on the chin with a hoof or manages to kick you in the shin. It *must* learn immediately that these things *do not* constitute civilized behavior, and that discomfort will always result from trying them.

Foals are so small and lovable that it sometimes takes a real act of will to reprimand them, even when they've earned it. When you find yourself backing off because "it just doesn't know any better," remind yourself of a few things:

First, it will *never* know any better if you don't teach it. The love and affection you give it will far offset the occasional well-timed whack you administer, and you will not be hurting it nearly to the extent that it can hurt you, even when it's accidental.

Second, your slap won't have nearly as much sting as the nip its dam gives it if it does something *she* doesn't like. A foal may be little, but it's still a pony, and its skin is nowhere near as sensitive as yours.

Third, consider that ponies don't excel at human-style logic, but they're great at causal relationships. Your saying, "Ow, that hurt me!" doesn't mean a thing to a pony. What *does* mean something is, "*If* you bite (kick, rear, etc.), *then* you get spanked, and it hurts." This thinking operates equally well in the positive arena: "*If* you come up to me when I call and let me hug you, *then* you get your itchiest unreachable places scratched, and that's so-o-o pleasant."

Finally, the lessons of foalhood aren't nearly as hard as those that come later in life, when learned bad behavior must be broken and replaced with good. Quite understandably, a spoiled yearling suddenly disciplined sharply for unruly behavior that it got away with at home is going to be confused. It will certainly rebel against unaccustomed reminders until it realizes that the struggle is useless and the handler determined. Far better to instill manners from the first day.

Foals have phenomenal memories, and they soak up knowledge like sponges. Don't hesitate to be quick with discipline when it's called for, but don't overdo it, and don't hold a grudge. Praise good behavior as immediately as you correct the inappropriate. This will give your foal a consistent start that will stand it in good stead throughout its life.

HALTERING AND LEADING

Foals can be haltered safely as early as a day or two after birth. Most will resist the strange thing being strapped to their faces, for which you can hardly blame them. As usual, the earlier it's done, the more likely they are to assume they were born that way. To keep the haltering from turning into a rodeo, *never* approach a foal directly from the front and expect to slip something over its nose, and try to do your initial lessons in a confined space rather than an open field or paddock. Use the hold position described above, and if possible have the foal backed gently up to a wall. With one arm wrapped around its chest, the other is free to slip the noseband of the halter over its muzzle and quickly pull the headstall over its ears. If the foal lunges forward, it'll lunge into the halter. If it backs away, hold on and go with it, *but don't wrestle with its head.* The halter is not yet a handle. Trying to control a very young foal by hanging onto its head can lead to its flipping over backwards or twisting its neck. In either case you run the risk of severe damage to the vertebrae that can lead to later potentially incurable neurological problems. Right now it's enough that the foal get used to wearing a halter, and having it put on and taken off.

Foals are best taught to lead with a bath towel around the base of the neck like a collar, and a firm hand on the rump. The towel won't chafe, and gives you a safe handle to steer with. Your hand on the rump propels the foal forward. Whether you teach it to lead by going behind or in front of the mare is entirely up to you, although if you're working alone the hand on the rump may also be holding your mare's lead, in which case propelling the foal along slightly in front of its dam is the easier route.

Letting foals run loose to follow their mothers is never a good idea. When they stray, which they inevitably do, their dams will become frantic and you'll quickly lose control of the situation. And if the foal gets "lost" (which means going even slightly off its accustomed path), it runs a terrible risk of becoming frightened and running headlong into fencing, the clothesline, the garden, the road, the tools you left lying around to be picked up later, and whatever else has managed to come between it and Mama. Anybody who has endured this scenario will tell you how terrifying and dangerous it is.

No matter what, *never turn a foal out wearing a nylon halter.* Freak accidents do occur in even the safest environments, and every year somebody has a horror story to tell about a foal that caught itself on a nylon halter and strangled, broke its neck, or hanged. Use only soft leather, which will stretch or break. Better yet, leave the halter off when the foal is turned out. In the early days it may take a bit of work to get it back on, once the foal is loose. Try catching it with the bath towel lead first; then, with one hand on the "collar" and the foal backed up to its dam, you should be able to slip the halter on fairly quickly, especially if you've already laid the groundwork for haltering in the stall.

As your foal gets the idea of leading, you can attach a shank to the halter and gradually begin using it either in conjunction with the towel or with a buttrope that drapes around the foal's hindquarters. Buttropes have the double advantage of helping to keep a recalcitrant foal moving forward while preventing it from throwing itself over backward. It also frees up one of your hands to lead Mama. Not all handlers like or need to use them, feeling that there is too much potential for the foal to get tangled in rope that's been allowed to go slack. They are, however, an extremely useful addition to any handler's repertoire of training aids when used properly.

If these early handling and leading lessons take place daily as a part of trips to and from the pasture, the foal should be an old pro by the time it's a month old. At this juncture it can also start to learn simple voice commands. "Whoa" and "Walk" are of greatest importance, obviously, and later you can add "Trot" and "Back." Well before weaning, a foal can be taught to stand for a few seconds as its dam walks away from it, to be led past her if she stops, and to walk away from its friends quietly. All this requires no more than five or ten minutes a day. Foals love learning, but their attention spans are very short. Daily lessons in the course of routine chores, rather than a heavily loaded hour spent every few weeks when you get around to it, will lay a solid and lasting foundation for future work.

THE WEANLING AND YEARLING

It's a myth to think that ponies too young to be backed are too young to do much of anything. Young ponies, like young children, are great mimics, and they love to learn to do the things they see their older friends doing. Breeders who take advantage of this delightfully useful trait can have a lot of fun with their youngsters without having to invest an enormous amount of time and effort in the proposition.

If your weanlings and yearlings are turned out with ponies that are groomed and ridden regularly, you'll rarely have to make an effort to *teach* them anything about grooming, handling, or tack. They'll be so interested in everything you're doing that you'll need a bomb to keep them out of the way. Go to pick up a brush, and you'll find it's been thrown into the water tub. Reach out to use the rubber currycomb on whomever you're about to ride, and you'll find a weanling's body wedged between yourself and your intended subject. Try to put on a bridle, and some yearling will stick its face into the headstall. *Use this eagerness and curiosity about life!* It's your best friend. Give the weanling a few strokes with the curry. Pretend to bridle the yearling and let it feel the headstall against its ears and chomp on the bit for a second, while you hold the bridle so that it can be backed out of easily. If a baby walks under the saddle when you lift it, rest it on its back for a second. All of these ordinary everyday things are a young pony's version of dressing up in Mom's jewels. These brief moments of experimentation in a totally informal setting will lead your youngsters to the idea that the grownup world is fine, and that handling and tack are fun.

If possible, let your youngsters be in a place where they can watch older ponies working and going down the road. They will find this fascinating, and when it comes their turn to go out they'll do it with pleasure and anticipation. Some youngsters will actually mimic the movements that they see their older cousins performing. Circles, changes of direction, transitions between paces, and even "schooling" over small obstacles for the sheer joy of it all become a part of their play.

When leading your youngster to and from the pasture, spend a few moments every day working on trotting, halting, standing, and walking on voice command. Pick up its feet in places where you might not ordinarily do so (but not until it's solid about picking up its feet in the stall). Drape yourself lightly over its back and pat its sides with your hands to simulate the feel of saddle, rider, girth, and legs. Vary your route to and from the barn so that you take little excursions that might include the drying laundry,

187

walking over the garden hose or across a piece of plastic, around the garage, and between your parked vehicles. Give it time to investigate things and process the information it gets.

Take it for walks down the road, to see the neighbor's dogs and the sheep in the next field. Lead it around the ring with you while you set up fences and drag poles and standards around. Teach it to lead behind you while you push the wheelbarrow. Teach it to walk beside you while you drag the muck bucket (empty and rattly) in your other hand. Teach it to pony beside your most solid citizen, and take it hacking with you. Teach it to pony beside your bicycle. Teach it to stand tied while being fed or groomed, then to stand cross-tied. Teach it about clippers, although not while the youngster is tied until it has become completely accustomed to them. Teach it to walk in and out of the trailer, one step at a time and rarely in one day. Give it rudimentary lessons in long-lining.

Don't, however, try to teach it to lunge, yet. Weanlings, yearlings, and even two-year-olds are still very loose-jointed. Too much work on a circle puts a lot of strain on immature joints, and if your youngster decides to hare around or buck and be fresh, it could easily injure itself. Moderate lunging should really wait until the two-year-old year, when the young pony is a bit more mature and already has a good grounding in the lessons suggested above.

A word of caution is in order here: Although this work is simple, basic, and usually nonstrenuous (within the parameters of youthful pony-type exuberance, that is to say), it should not be dealt with alone by a young child. Ponies, no matter what their age, learn very quickly who can make an order stick and who can be cowed into believing that a certain tractor really *does* eat ponies or that a certain bush really *should* be avoided. If you have kids that ride, and if this is one of the reasons you're breeding ponies in the first place, the best of all possible worlds is to have them helping you with all facets of the operation, training included. It's fun, educational, and very satisfying, and helps them to grow into adults who will have the knowledge and experience to become the next generation's solid horsepersons. But your eye on the proceedings will make sure that no insurmountable problems are being encountered or inadvertent bad habits being learned.

Foals, broodstock, and youngsters alike can benefit from the odd trip into public. It gives them the opportunity to see and get used to new things, like Connemaras Happy Ness and Armful of Tiger Lilies. *Photo: Melissa Kelly.*

OUT IN PUBLIC

The occasional excursion to a breed show or a small local show gives you another opportunity to put some early polish on your young ponies, as well as giving them a taste of what life may have in store for them. Although taking foals on the road with their dams isn't everybody's idea of a good time, it's actually fairly simple if you take a few simple precautions. The first is that the mare travels tied, the foal travels loose. This way it can position itself in the most comfortable way—which may be traveling frontwards, backwards, or even sideways—with Mama for support and the milk source readily available if it gets hungry or worried. Next, the front of the trailer must have a solid partition to keep the foal from scooting under the chest bar and getting stuck or tangled in any way. If you're handy, you can cut a piece of plywood to fit and attach it with bolts or snaps so that it won't fall.

They can also gain valuable ring experience, as shown by Sig and Carol Swanberg and their young Haflingers. *Photo: Stan Phaneuf.*

If you're no good at this sort of project, you can have your local auto body wizard customize exactly the kind of partition you want. Or you can take the route of stacking hay bales across the front, tying them securely in place so that your mare won't be able to knock them over in the process of trying to eat as much of them as possible during the trip. Whichever route you choose, it *must* be secure, safe, and able to withstand the pressures of being pawed at, leaned on, and chewed. Anything that can come loose, or that can be climbed on, or that a foal can get its head or foot through, is both frightening and very, very dangerous.

Some people prefer to remove the trailer's center partition altogether to give mare and foal more room to maneuver. Others prefer to swing the ramp end over so that there's more support for the mare, if she needs it, and not quite so much room for the foal to get up a head of steam. Either system works.

Finally, don't for a second think that your foal won't try to jump out over the closed ramp; it might. If you have upper doors, close them. If you have a rain curtain, try to secure it in such a way that it offers a solid-looking barrier without cutting off all possibility of air circulation in the trailer.

There is some division of opinion as to whether foals are best loaded before or after their dams. Some blithely maintain that if you load the mare, the foal will follow her on. Others maintain that it more often leads to a balky foal that refuses to follow and a frantic mare trying to unload herself again as quickly as possible to get back to her baby. In this case, loading the foal first is the better policy. Once in, the foal's curiosity at its surroundings will keep it occupied until the mare is on. A handful of grain will certainly help. And the mare will be much happier being able to see her foal.

Traveling with yearlings can be a nightmare if undertaken without the benefit of early acclimatization to the trailer, and even sometimes with it. These young orangutans are the ones most likely to try leaping over the chest bar and out through the escape door, which is one of any breeder's more terrifying nightmares. Early training on and off the trailer, with the ramp lifted and let down again, and even a few very short trips with a steady and quiet companion, can help considerably in getting the youngster used to the sights and sounds of the trailer's enclosed space. If you have an especially nervy pony, *don't* force the issue right away, no matter how badly you want to take it to its first show. An unhappy early trailering experience can be responsible for untold problems later on. Yearling ponies are still small and not very heavy, and can certainly be muscled into a trailer by a couple of hefty and determined men. Nothing is gained by this, however. Getting it loaded again to go home will be worse, and every time force is used the problem will just compound itself until you have a pony that "doesn't load." These ponies are far better off given the extra time they need to be relaxed about the whole loading and traveling process. *The time spent instilling good habits is far shorter in the long run than the time spent trying to break bad ones later on.* Even with your quiet ones, it pays to have these early trips taken in company with an experienced traveler. The youngsters will be comforted by their steadiness, and they will also copy good behavior and learn manners from it.

Once at the showground, don't simply throw your pony in a stall, put up the stall guard, and leave it there for the weekend. The point of this exercise is not so much showing as it is sight-seeing. Let the youngster go everywhere with you. Take it to the warm-up ring and let it get used to the crowds and noise and chaos. Take it to the concession stands and let it look at the little plastic flags flapping in the breeze. Stand it under the loud-speakers and let it get used to hearing the weird noises that come out of them. Give it time to absorb all these new sights and sounds. Keep it out as long as it stays interested and appears to be handling everything without being overloaded. Then put it away with some hay and some praise and let it have some peace and quiet. Put a stall guard up over its door if you plan on leaving it unattended for awhile. It's fine to give it the opportunity to hang its head out of its stall and ogle at all the interesting and amazing things happening around it, but if you leave it's wise not to tempt fate. Overexcited young ponies are perfectly capable of jumping out of stalls to try to find their friends.

A busy, crowded showground is not the place to teach your pony something brand new, like tying or lunging or being backed for the first time. The things it has to look at are more than enough input to process at one time. All you're asking is that it learn to look to you for signals on what to do and how to behave, just as it does at home. In this way you'll continue to instill the trust and obedience your ponies will require later in whatever discipline the future holds for them.

MOVING RIGHT ALONG

Most breeders try to get youngstock sold as young as possible, but every now and then all of us wind up with a few three-year-olds around. While weanlings, yearlings, and sometimes two-year-olds can be sold "on spec" for their future potential, a three-year-old is expected to show a buyer what it might have to offer as a legitimate prospect in its discipline. Most people aren't willing to pay top dollar for an animal that's still standing around in the field at this age, no matter how fancy its heritage is. Those that say they're willing to look at green ponies generally mean those that lack mileage, not those that lack rudimentary training.

An average three-year-old is physically and mentally prime for being gently broken and started under saddle, a process that should hold few major surprises, if you've done the early groundwork discussed above. The question is whether you can undertake the schooling yourself, or whether it will be best left to a professional trainer. There are benefits and drawbacks to either proposition. Good professionals don't come cheap, and if you're on a tight budget the temptation is often to do without. On the other hand, a young pony's early introduction to ridden work is critical to its future as a performer. Riders of very green ponies must be imbued with legs of iron, saintly patience, and a constant level of tact and cheerful firmness in the face of obstacles that range from the mildly infuriating (it just started to pour down rain and the pony is convinced that gremlins live under the last bridge between you and a dry barn) to the terrifying (a large rattling truck loaded with garbage has just crashed over a bump in the road and sent plastic milk bottles and old newspapers flying out of the back into your path). The situations that a young pony will accept and those that send it over the edge are difficult, if not impossible, to predict, and they may vary from day to day. Your youngsters will learn how to behave in all these new situations *from their rider's reactions and cues.* If in the face of all available horrors the rider is relaxed, encouraging, firm, and in control, the pony will learn to accept, respect, trust, and obey. The rider who is unbalanced, timid, short-tempered, aggressive, or in a hurry will only prove to the pony that it had better take control of the situation itself, since clearly nobody else is looking out for its well-being.

If you and your children are good, solid intermediates who already take lessons regularly, there isn't any reason why you can't do a lot of the work of breaking your three-year-olds under supervision and with advice. Alternately, you may be able to hire a good local pony clubber or other accomplished young rider to help get your ponies started as an after school or summer job.

Make sure these people have references you trust, and arrange to watch them ride and handle their own or their trainers' ponies before turning them loose on yours. And no matter how keen, hardworking, and desperate she is, the girl down the road who has "ridden for years at summer camp" *doesn't count* as a good choice for your young ponies' training. A talented, sensible, scopey young pony can be turned into a balky, spoiled, frightened one in a matter of weeks by handling that is well meant but ignorant. People are hurt daily by even the kindest and quietest green pony in an unforeseen situation that gets out of hand. The old adage that green ponies and green riders don't mix obviously has its exceptions, but it's wisest to pay attention to it when thinking of the best grounding for yours.

You may decide to go the route of sending them to a trainer whom you trust and respect for at least month or two of consistent work. A good professional sees a tremendous number of people in the course of a season, and the visibility your pony will receive in the hands (and barn) of a reputable trainer may mean the difference between a sale and another winter of feeding a pony that isn't going anywhere fast. The value added by solid basic training in the hands of a person whose livelihood depends on turning out well-schooled ponies can easily offset its initial cost.

FINALLY . . .

Handling stock of any age requires consistency above all else. You can't allow a pony to chew on you sometimes and not others, or walk all over you at home but not at the shows. You can't expect it to lead quietly if all it's done is follow its dam or its friends to and from the pasture. You can't expect it to stand for the vet and the farrier if it won't stand for you. You can't punish it for something it has never learned without expecting it to be resentful. You can't expect it to learn to do anything cheerfully if you don't praise and make much of it when it does the things you ask. When you give a pony of any age mixed messages, it will almost certainly become confused and sulky or rebellious, and you'll end up with a pony that would rather fight you than be your willing partner. This is as unfortunate as it is unnecessary.

Nearly all the bad manners picked up by ponies began as poor early handling. Young ponies especially are smart, curious, and eager to please. Even a few minutes a day spent in their company will teach them all they need to know to be well-socialized animals with good prospects as useful riding or driving ponies. Obviously, this is as good for your reputation as a breeder as it is for the future of your ponies. But it's also a great excuse for slowing down a little and really enjoying your youngsters to the greatest possible degree, which is, after all, a major reason for getting into this business in the first place.

Of Manners, Mares, and Stallions

Overworked and understaffed pony breeders have a tendency to let their mares and stallions go virtually unhandled for long periods of time. The reasoning is generally that there isn't time to work with everybody (very true, usually), and that since the "old folks" aren't going to go anywhere in particular, it doesn't much matter whether their manners and obedience are right up to snuff. Besides, they're mature animals now, so they'll remember their early education when you need them to, right? Well, not really.

Ponies are very good at being wild. After all, it was their advanced instincts for survival as much as their genetic hardiness that allowed them to thrive for centuries more or less untouched by humans. This is one of the reasons that we appreciate them, but it can be a drawback if they aren't periodically brought in to be civilized. Mares and stallions that are handled only when wormed, visited by the vet or farrier, or during breeding and foaling (all very high-stress situations) quickly "go bush," and can become bossy and opinionated when you need to do something to or with them.

In the case of broodmares, it's a simple matter to bring them into stalls occasionally to get out of the heat or bugs and spend a few moments grooming them and checking them for bites, nicks, and so on. Ordinary routines like this, coupled with the insistence that they not walk all over you or push you around while being led and handled, results in mares that remain kindly and easy to deal with.

Stallions are a bit more labor-intensive. If yours is being groomed and ridden, or even groomed and led to and from pastures daily, chances are good that you'll be staying on top of his behavior pretty well, and stallions whose days include some sort of nonbreeding, performance-type activity are generally much happier than those relegated to lonely and boring paddocks all their lives. A breeding stallion that is haltered only for vetting, trimming, or breeding, on the other hand, can become rank and difficult.

As maintained throughout this section, a few minutes spent working on your stallion's manners in the course of your daily routine can make all the difference in the world. Use the time spent going from barn to paddock in brushing up his showring skills. Vary the walk by going through some transitions to trot, halt, stand, trot again. Put a chain over his nose to keep him from dragging you around. If he doesn't pull, it won't put pressure on him. If he does, a few sharp tugs while you tell him to walk on, stand, or whatever it is that you want, will bring his attention back to you. If he shoves you (a favorite stallion trick) slap him open handed on the side of the face and say *"No!"* very firmly. Carry a bat. If he tries to rear, buck, or bite, use it, *but never on the head.* Repeat *"No!"* as you use discipline, then follow it immediately with whatever command you want him to listen to. As soon as he pays attention to you and does as you ask, praise him mightily. *Your stallion must pay attention to you at all times.* If he has no respect for you in the course of daily handling, he will be impossible when it comes time to tease and breed.

It's wise to monitor your own behavior to make sure that you deliver only as much discipline is required, and no more. Most stallions have an inborn sense of justice, and when they learn where the boundaries are, they will respect them (and you). Being stallions, they will also test those boundaries periodically to make sure you're committed to them, but this generally calls for no more response than a growled warning. A stallion that is beaten for every small move will quickly become resentful and nasty. One that is disciplined erratically if at all will be spoiled and obstreperous. Both are unpleasant at best and unsafe at worst.

Although strict discipline is essential, your stallion needs most of all to associate you with pleasant experiences. Many stallions spend so much time alone that they're starved for physical attention. One way to maintain a good relationship with yours is to give him a good grooming to scratch all of his itchy spots and help keep his skin and coat healthy. Ponies are gregarious creatures, and use grooming as a social, as much as a practical, occasion. This works to your own benefit if you approach it in the same manner and use the time you spend doing it to build a better understanding with your ponies.

If your stallion doesn't have a performance career, he'll still thrive on being taken out periodically to be lunged, long-lined, or even going for a hand walk to see the countryside. If he gets used to thinking of you in the context of situations that are fun and pleasant, his behavior in all areas will begin to relax and improve. This will stand you in good stead both on-farm and in the event that you should decide to take him out in public.

Chapter

12

MARKETING YOUR STOCK

Marketing is serious business. Your ability to get your ponies into the eye and mind of the pony-buying public is going to be important, if you expect to sell anything or to attract outside mares to your stallion. And although this may consist largely of getting your youngstock (and even some of your broodstock) out in public to develop good performance or in-hand records, it also requires regular advertising, and the possibility of brochures, public relations pieces, and videos. Added to this is the importance of building a good reputation, which is sometimes less a function of producing winning ponies than it is one of good record-keeping, nicely handled and well-kept ponies, and a friendly, knowledgeable, *honest* manner with potential customers and other breeders. The good news is that you don't have to be a tycoon to develop a creative image that enhances the public view of what your farm and ponies have to offer.

THE PERFORMANCE ANGLE

Nothing will build your farm's reputation faster than a pony that is competing regularly and successfully. Obviously, the person who has a professional trainer and is out campaigning week after week is going to be seen by a tremendous number of potential customers. Many breeders feel that the money spent for this type of exposure, especially for a stallion, is money well spent. Even if you only go out a few times a year and are your own trainer, groom, and jockey (or your children are the jockeys and you're everything else), your well-behaved, talented, nicely turned out ponies will have a positive effect on the people who see them. You don't have to win all the time. It's enough to be consistent and look like you're having a good time. If your ponies also look like they're having a good time, and if they clearly enjoy their work, the word will get around, people will come up to chat and ask about your pony, and in time they may turn out to be clients.

Breeding shows are useful, too. For one thing, they provide a great avenue for getting broodmares and youngstock out in the public eye for some experience and a bit of polishing up. For another, it gives spectators a chance to see what sort of animals it is you're producing. Again, winning is nice, but it isn't all that important on a cosmic scale. If you're successfully breeding the kind of ponies you want to ride or drive, and if your ponies reflect the pride and care you've taken in them, they will attract a following from people with similar tastes regardless of in-hand pinnings. In time, your farm name will be linked with a certain stamp of pony that a certain type of person has been looking high and low for.

However you choose to do your showing, be sure that you always arrive with your ponies looking their best. They deserve to be clean, glowing with health, and well turned out. You should be well turned out, too. If you wander into a ring with a pony that's just been dragged in from the pasture and has clearly been taught nothing about rudimentary ring manners, and if your attitude expresses the idea that you think this whole process is totally silly, you'll be treated that way by both the judge and the people standing on the rail. If you hate showing and it really isn't fun for you, don't do it. There are plenty of other ways to market ponies.

THE PRINT AD

For most of us, glossy four-color ads in national magazines will remain as much a fantasy as riding for the USET show-jumping squad. Yet print advertising will still form the backbone of even the most limited marketing budget. And if it is going to succeed in its goal (which is to bring people to your farm), it's got to be good. This means that it's brief, provides a few critical pieces of information in the smallest number of words, and has a photo that is large, clear, shows your pony in the best possible light, and has enough action that it immediately draws a reader's eye.

It's amazing how simple this sounds—and how few people pay attention to it. A browse through a few copies of your favorite equine publications reveals that many ads suffer from too many words, photos that are blurred or show animals poorly posed and badly turned out, and a size too small to give any idea of the quality of the pony advertised.

Studies have shown that the average reader takes about three to seven *seconds* to scan a magazine page, settling only on the things that "zap" the eye, or make a positive impact that encourages them to look more closely at a photo or its accompanying copy. Creating an eye-stopping ad thus becomes your first priority.

Begin planning your ad campaign by deciding what you can afford to pay over the course of a year. Many breeders recommend spending the equivalent of one to two stud fees as a base from which to start. This may not sound like a lot of money in terms of the cost of advertising, but it can still be a stretch for the average small breeder with grain to buy. The trick is to maximize the effect of that budgeted amount.

First, try to identify the scope of your market. Will most of your ponies sell in your region, so that regional advertising without a national focus will be successful, or do you anticipate a broader market? If you stand a stallion, will you be offering breedings via artificial insemination that merit advertising to a national audience? Do you expect that your response will be largely breed-specific so that advertising in your breed's journal will provide all the exposure you need? And is there a magazine that will have enough overlap in its readership to provide you with an image that will be widely seen by other breeders as well as a broad selection of people in your targeted market group on both the regional and national level? Many magazines devote at least one issue per year focusing on either a specific breed or on ponies as a whole. These are often good places to advertise, as the people who pick them up off the stand are likely to be buying them for those specialized contents, and can be expected to hold onto them for awhile. Subscribers also tend to keep these issues for future reference, which automatically gives your ad more clout and a greater shelf life. Many breeders maintain that they have received calls from people who read an ad in one of these issues, rediscovered it several years later, and chose that moment to call.

Next, decide on the optimum size of ad for your budget. One breeder may find that in a national magazine, a two-inch ad with an attractive logo (with name, address, and phone number attached, along with the name of the breed you're advertising) and a great head shot of an outstanding pony will bring in numerous calls. Another may find that one-sixth page, either horizontal (spread across two columns of a three-column, $8^1/_2$-by-11-inch page) or vertical (one column wide but longer), will give the ideal balance between photo and copy. In a regional magazine, you might stretch to something twice that size for about the same price. If you have more to spend, many magazines now contain "marketplace" sections where, for a moderate fee, breeders can run a very attractive small ad with a good photo all year long.

Public awareness of a name or a logo will grow for something that they see advertised as little as three or four times a year. Even advertising twice annually, in carefully selected issues of magazines likely to give you the greatest possible exposure to your market, will frequently be enough to begin the process of "brand recognition," especially if you have a nice logo to go with it.

A logo can be as simple or as elaborate as you can make it. You may want to do it yourself, if you have any artistic talent, or

Your pony doesn't have to be braided and turned out to the nines to make a good advertising impression if it is as clean, well groomed, and nicely presented as Connemara Montully's Son (Montully Man x Marconi's Stormy Rebel). *Photo: May Medley.*

perhaps you know an art student who would love to create one for you. There are also some wonderful graphics books widely available in bookstores and art supply stores that are full of non-copyrighted designs, borders, and alphabets that you can cut out and use as a part of your package. If you work with a personal computer, there are programs that have many attractive borders and logos, as well, or you can design your own using one of the many straightforward art or works programs.

The thing to remember is that, although you may be designing your ad on $8\,^{1}/_{2}$-by-11-inch paper (regular size) or $5\,^{1}/_{2}$-by-$8\,^{1}/_{2}$-inch paper (the former folded in half), the finished ad will be reduced considerably to fit a small space in a magazine. When designing a logo or border, try to keep it as uncluttered and clear as possible so that it will still look sharp when it's about a quarter of the size you're starting with.

The photos you choose to represent your ponies and your farm are going to be the single factor that will cause readers to pause and read your ad or turn the page, never to come back. Don't by any means use that slightly out-of-focus shot you took of your stallion galloping around his field last spring when he was covered with mud and not quite shed out and the grass hadn't started growing yet. Don't use any shot of a pony that cuts off its feet or shows its neck turned in an odd position or its legs pointing every which way. And don't ever use a photo of your pony over fences in which its form is anything but perfect. The public won't care that it's a great big fence, nor will they know that it was the one fence all year that your pony jumped poorly. All they'll see is a pony looking really bad over a fence. Far better to use a very nice shot of a pony looking wonderful over a small one. It's the form that will impress. The same is true for any performance shot, in any discipline.

The best photos to use are generally those that have been taken at a show by a professional photographer. Photographers are usually happy to give you permission to use the shots you buy for farm advertising purposes, as long as the photo is properly credited to them. It's wise to ask first, however. If you intend to take your own photos, make sure that you have time to turn your ponies out as if they were going to a show. Their coats should be clean and gleaming, neither unshed nor parched by the sun. Manes and tails should be, if not braided, at least washed and thoroughly brushed out. If you're after traditional conformation shots, the pony should wear a bridle. Have a handler pose it properly, with the fore and hindleg closest to the camera slightly framing those farthest from it. A pony leaning over its front legs, or with the foreleg nearest the camera behind the farther one, will look straight shouldered. Likewise, your own stance is important. Try to position yourself so that the camera's lens is about level with a point just below the pony's withers. If you shoot from above that (a tall person photographing a short pony), it will look like a Dachshund. If you shoot from downhill, it will look oddly long-legged.

When shooting, try to find a neutral background that is not going to result in your photos being ruined by telephone poles, drying laundry, manure piles, stacked lumber, assorted children's toys, or your parked vehicles appearing to sprout out of the subject's head or back. A light-colored barn wall is ideal for a darker-colored pony. A background of a neat hedge or other neutral dark area is great for a grey or light-colored one. An open field or paddock is fine, too, if you are careful of what's in the immediate background.

If you want to shoot movement, the same rules apply, with the addition that you must position yourself in a spot where a good long trot is possible without abrupt turns that can unbalance the pony or cause it to look strangely angled. And keep shooting; an entire role of film may yield only one or two shots worth saving.

Choose performance photos that show your pony doing something it excels at, like this one of Welsh Cob Nesscliffe Sunrise and owner-breeder India Haynes. *Photo: Toni Mayr.*

Problems may arise when you use color film for a black-and-white ad. Color can be used, but it does require care in the contrast of the final product. Red, for instance, will read as black to a camera's eye, so your black pony against a dark red barn—which looks lovely in color—will come out looking like a dark blob against a darker blob when turned into a black-and-white halftone.

The final element of your ad is the written part, called copy. Before you paste anything in, write down everything you want to say. Then cut it in half. Then cut it in half again. Maybe even again. The fewer and stronger words you use, the better. You obviously must include your farm name, address, phone, the breed(s) you specialize in, and whether there are photos, a video, or a brochure. You need to identify the pony in the photo and state its particulars, including whether it's at stud or for sale and for how much. You need to state whether there are more where these came from, and *maybe* you'll have room to mention a couple of famous names that were sired by your stallion or bred on your farm. And that's all. *Let your photos do the talking.* There will be time for hyperbole when you get interested people on the farm to see for themselves.

VIDEOS AND BROCHURES

Three modern inventions that have had a tremendous amount of importance for the small breeder are the video camera, the color laser copier, and the personal computer. Armed with these tools, anybody can provide professional-looking advertising support materials on a relative shoestring.

Videos of broodstock and ponies for sale have become common, but there are many really bad videos out there showing nothing but hours' worth of grazing ponies in a landscape, the brief sight of a stallion's tail going by at great speed, or that time-honored view of a curious pony sticking its hairy nose up to the camera lens. Good videos, like nice photos, require forethought and planning. They can certainly be informal, but they should look a little better than something you raced out to try to grab quickly on your way to work in the morning. To begin with, it helps to write yourself a little script so that you'll know what you want to say and how you want to highlight your ponies. You'll begin by identifying any pony with its age, size, breeding, level of training (if it's for sale), winnings (if any), and successful off-spring. You might add a quick anecdote or two describing the pony's personality, temperament, or ability to pass on certain of its quirks and attributes to its foals.

All of this can be taking place while the pony is being filmed both standing and in motion, or while being ridden, with periods of silence in between to let the viewer watch the pony. Try to rehearse before you start filming. Nothing's worse than receiving a video replete with a domestic argument over the way a pony is standing or moving (or not standing or moving, as the case may be).

If you don't have a video recorder, there are places that will rent them. Better yet, there is probably a video nut in your neigh-borhood who, for a small fee, will be happy to come and film your ponies with you. Spend some time explaining *exactly* what you're after. The results will be a credit to your ponies.

If you have video footage of your ponies garnered from shows, sale videos, and more informal home studies that include kids, pets and ponies all interacting, you can mark the passages you like most, take the lot to a specialty place that offers editing, and make a visually entertaining and very appeal-ing ad for your whole farm. This is obviously not cheap, but it's a great potential selling point, and the person editing the mate-rial can offer voice-overs (your voice talking over the action to introduce various segments), fade-ins and fade-outs, and all sorts of modern techniques that will probably not break your budget wide open.

A quality brochure is also an effective way to advertise your farm and ponies. For one thing, brochures are cheap to mail and very portable so that you can carry them with you wherever you go. You can hand them to admirers of your ponies, pin them on the walls of your local tack and feed store, and write notes on them to people who've called about the attractive ad they just saw in the last issue of their favorite equine publication.

Creating a brochure used to be a pretty expensive proposition, requiring a lot of screening of photos as well as layout costs and the actual printing. Then, to get the whole thing at a reasonable price, you had to order so many copies that you still had 150 left at the end of five years, by which time they were hopelessly outdated. The advent of the color copier and of desktop publishing in its many forms has changed all this. For photocopying, you can use as many or as few photos as will fit on the page attractively, setting them in place with a glue stick. On the back side (which can't be color but will copy in black and white) you can put the logo, address and phone, pertinent information about the ponies, and whatever glowing things you've written about your ponies, still leaving space for a brief note. Your local print shop can show you how to go about all this. By the single copy it can run around $5, which may seem like a lot. But if you order more than twelve (this may vary from place to place), you can usually get a substantial discount and bring the per-piece price down to about what you'd pay for a commercial greeting card. It has the added benefit that you can order only what you'll need for a year or two, and it can be changed at any point because it doesn't require professionally screened photos, which can cost $10 each. In addition, the copy you store in your personal computer can be updated at will so that you're never faced with mailing anything out of date.

MAKING USE OF FREE PUBLICITY

Local papers, both dailies and weeklies, are frequently looking for what's known as "fillers," or small news items and general interest pieces to add to the breadth and appeal of their publications. If you have any writing expertise, or if you know somebody who does, the occasional piece about your farm and its special activities—whether a big award won or a visitor from a foreign country, or a pony imported or exported, or even an open barn to see foals in the spring—can help to raise public awareness about who you are and what you're doing.

Your Own Best Advertisement

Your own friendliness and helpfulness, the quality and manageability of your ponies, and the physical appearance of your place will be the things that bring people to your farm a second time or that will cause them to pass your name to others. You don't have to live in a showplace, as long as your ponies are obviously healthy and happy and you maintain a barn that is clean and inviting to visitors. Organization is a big plus, too. It will always serve you well to keep meticulous vet records on all of your ponies, as well as a full pedigree chart with whatever annotations are appropriate, and good performance and breeding records of your ponies' parents and siblings. Buyers appreciate being able to know as much as possible about the pony they're about to spend a considerable amount of money on. The existence of excellent records presented to them in a format that's easy to read and refer back to is a major plus in giving them a sense of security about these major decisions, as well as immediately answering many of the questions that will inevitably be raised about any of the above-mentioned topics. It also illustrates a level of care and concern on your part that will eventually speak far louder than any amount of paid advertising can ever do.

So will your attitude toward other breeders. Never be afraid to send people elsewhere if you really don't have what they're looking for. There is no place in a small world for the kind of backbiting that sets one breeder against another and confuses the innocent buyers who are simply looking for the best pony to suit their needs. By all means encourage your potential customers to look at the stock of other breeders before making up their minds. If they come back to you—as many will—you'll know that they made their decision armed with greater knowledge than they had when they started. As any business owner can tell us, getting people though the door once is easy. Getting them to come back, and to bring their friends with them, is what makes a successful operation. This all adds up to the idea of service, both on behalf of the ponies we believe in and on behalf of the people that we hope will become their loving (and maybe even winning) owners.

Chapter

13

PONIES ARE NOT
JUST KID'S STUFF

Not all adults want to ride something that requires a stepladder to mount or partnership in a grain company to feed. Many people who have trouble enough juggling the constraints of time and finances caused by jobs, marriages, and children and who *still* want to enjoy riding frequently find themselves leaning toward animals that are smaller, thriftier, tougher, and more adaptable to less-than-ideal living conditions than their larger cousins. On the other hand, who of us wants a clunker? We want the best of both worlds: attractiveness, a forward attitude, and a good athlete wrapped in a body that's easy to maintain and encompassing a balanced mind. A pony that is a good example of its breed or cross has the ability, character, and looks to provide the ideal solution, with the added plus of being able to double as a sensible and attractive children's mount when called on to do so.

And while it's all too true that those who ride over fences find obstacles looking larger and more imposing from the back of a pony than from that of a horse, many adults freely admit to feeling far safer over a large fence in trappy conditions on a pony that they know will stay upright no matter what they do than on

Not every adult wants an immense horse. The Haflinger Fancy Free N.T.F. (Napoleon Esquire x Fortuna) does everything Donna Messier wants her to. *Photo: Stan Phaneuf.*

a bigger animal that may not be as good or careful a jumper. Or, as one endurance rider said of her ponies, "They'll always look out for number one. I like that—it means all I have to do is stay in the middle, and I'll be fine!"

Ponies have thus existed as the ideal weekend warrior for many people for many years. The adults who ride, drive, and swear by them have likewise represented a very committed minority, especially visible in foxhunting, combined training, combined driving, and competitive trail. In these areas, ponies as mounts for adult riders have historically enjoyed considerable success. The gradually increasing acceptance and popularity of ponies as mounts for amateur adults in these and almost all other disciplines is reflected in the numbers of all-breeds awards offered by such organizations as the U.S. Combined Training Association (USCTA) and the U.S. Dressage Federation (which

210

All-breeds competitions have opened new avenues for adults riding ponies like Custusha's Cashel Rock. *Connemara Country File.*

instituted the first all-breed award program in the early 1980s), as well as the numbers of ponies that fill American Driving Society (ADS) pony divisions at nearly all of their competitions. Both the USCTA and the ADS estimate that anywhere from 20 percent to 25 percent of their adult members compete with ponies or pony crosses.

The positive image and expanded following these good performers and their owners have created translates to a growing market for breeders interested in providing ponies for a burgeoning population of adult riders. Those who want to tap into it would do well to talk with and observe serious amateurs as well as respected professionals in targeted disciplines to find out more about what is liked or disliked about the various types of ponies that compete in specific regions and why. Opinions and acceptance vary greatly from place to place, and the responses you get can be edifying, ranging from utter dislike for any pony under any circumstances when ridden by anyone but a child, to amused tolerance and provisional consideration, to warm regard.

As amateur and all-breeds divisions prosper, however, and as more adults ride ponies, small horses, and odd-colored animals, more and more professionals and judges are accepting of the idea of adults riding ponies, albeit with a few caveats.

Chief of these is suitability of pony to rider, with trainers and judges alike nearly unanimous in their assertion that ponies should not be weighed down by large or heavy adult riders. They must be in balance with one another visually. Just as it's physically and mechanically unfair to expect a pony to carry a tall, heavy adult around a course of fences (even if that adult is exceptionally well balanced), it's unrealistic to expect an adult amateur rider to learn to maintain a steady balance or position on an animal that is so comparatively small that it feels like it's going to shoot the rider over its disappearing head every time it lands over a fence, jump out from underneath the rider with every step that isn't absolutely straight forward, or whose sides disappear somewhere under the rider's upper calf and leave his or her legs unsupported and more or less useless. Any pony under consideration by an adult should thus give the sense of having plenty of body to get a leg on and a good length of rein so that the rider feels that there's a lot in front of him or her.

Issues such as scope (the athletic ability to be able to achieve a desired level of performance) and stride (the ability to "do the distances" between fences comfortably, as well as being able to adjust easily for the lengthening and shortening of stride that are demanded to some degree in every competitive discipline), come second in any list of concerns. Attention to a good foundation is all that's required in most cases to enhance natural talent, and one internationally renowned dressage rider maintains staunchly that her great success on half a dozen pony breeds can be duplicated with any breed, if she is allowed to train it properly.

Size a drawback? Here, 14.1-hand Connemara Balius Kerry Blue (Gilnocky Drumcliffe x Polaris Suzanne) successfully competes at open preliminary in combined training with Lee Webster. *Photo: Ed Lawrence Photography.*

WHEN PONIES COMPETE WITH HORSES: SPECIAL CONSIDERATIONS IN DRESSAGE AND OVER FENCES

Riding ponies over courses with distances set for the longer strides of an average horse (usually seen as 16+ hands and largely Thoroughbred) provides riders with a very specific set of challenges. This is also true for dressage, where warmblood movement is the standard by which many performances are measured, especially at the lower levels. While in a perfect world all ponies would be born with long, reaching action at the trot and level, twelve-foot strides when they canter, nature has ordained that they be as individual in their build and movement as people are. And while it isn't uncommon to find a pony whose movement makes your heart beat faster, reality has it that the

213

average 14.2-hand pony just won't have the length of stride its 16.2-hand cousins do without some effort to improve on nature's gifts.

There is nothing in the way of a nice pony putting in a correct, forward, and fluid dressage test or a smooth, flowing hunter round, however. The current popularity of musical kurs and their emphasis on artistry as well as technicality has given many ponies a place in which to shine in dressage. And the lower-level jumper divisions, with their emphasis on timed jump-offs, give a really handy pony that can cut corners and turn on a dime a great advantage. The key to success in these and other venues is a training program that will create a pony that is forward, balanced, and flexible.

Whether your goal is dressage or the hunter ring, your basic work will be the same. Negotiating a flowing jumping round, after all, has less to do with getting over the fences than with what happens between them, and very few ponies have unattractive form over fences, being naturally round and generally happy, careful, scopey jumpers that won't willingly hit anything. Whatever your discipline, then, your first attention will be the basic tenets of dressage training, or creating a pony that is calm, forward, and straight. There are a number of very good books available that can outline the exact process of this basic schooling in far more detail than we are able to here. (See the appendix for a partial list.) In general, however, the pattern of your

Proper attention to basic schooling can enhance any breed's ability to perform well in any discipline, as evidenced by Norwegian Fjord F. G. Rasken (Modellen x Rosita) and trainer Janice Schreurrs Conlon.

The Essential School Figures

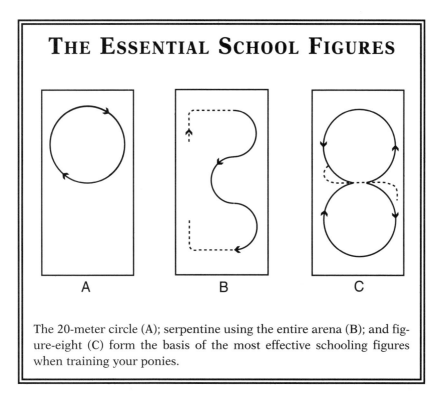

The 20-meter circle (A); serpentine using the entire arena (B); and figure-eight (C) form the basis of the most effective schooling figures when training your ponies.

ring work will consist of many 20-meter circles and straightforward changes of rein in large figure-eights or big, loopy serpentines. Your focus will be on maintaining a steady pace, a proper bend, and enough strides in a straight line when changing the rein to organize a change of bend to the other direction without allowing your pony to haul you into the corner, flatten out, or lean on you. All of these frequently seen habits are a sign that you aren't riding enough from your leg and seat, and need to be riding your pony more from back to front rather than pulling on its head to try to get it into the kind of package you want.

Your first goal with this kind of work is to achieve *relaxation of the back*, without which your pony can't possibly lengthen, shorten, or adjust its stride. As you work, also try to develop a sense of rhythm, which goes hand-in-hand with relaxation. One way to do this is to sing nursery school songs to yourself.

Native ponies can also hold their own in demanding sports like competitive trail riding. Connemara Springledge Irish Whiskey (Springledge Bantry Bay x *Dublin Grey) and Dr. Marian Molthan completed the Western States Trail Ride (Tevis Cup) nine times. *Connemara Country File photo.*

It may sound silly, but "The Grand Old Duke of York" and "The Green Grass Grows All Around" are two songs that are ideally suited to trotting rhythms. If you sing them out loud, not only will it stabilize your posting rhythm, it will also affect your pony. You'll find it trotting more and more in the rhythm of the song.

Add upward and downward transitions between all three paces as well as some work on basic lateral movements such as leg yielding to further encourage your pony to move forward more responsively, step further underneath itself with its hindlegs, and become more flexible. Troubleshoot your own position and effectiveness by listening to what the pony is telling you. Is it lugging, or pulling like a train? Ponies are strong for their size, and when they build up a head of steam or decide to pull you along as a way of avoiding the aids, you can easily feel that you're mounted on a rhinoceros. If this is happening, slow your

Pony hitches are a popular feature at fairs all over North America. Here, Joel Hempel drives his team of Norwegian Fjord mares.

trotting rhythm by posting a little higher than usual and a little slower than the pony's pace. And stop pulling back. Use your legs more to push your pony forward into the bridle. Use half halts to gather the energy. Squeeze and release with your hand instead of wrestling with the pony's head. Think of it as an exercise in simple physics: Your pony outweighs you by a considerable amount, and your weight pulling against its is a losing proposition. Activating your seat and leg to drive the pony forward into an elastic hand, however, will result in the pony coming up against its *own* weight in the bridle. Your hands steady, contain, or release the energy according to the amount of forward motion or collection you want to create.

As it begins to listen, loosen its back, relax its stride, and use its hindlegs more actively, you'll find your pony feeling much better balanced and far more adjustable. This adds up to more power from the "engine" when you need it as well as a pony that is lighter in the hand and far more sensitive in the "steering department."

Many pony riders suffer from the delusion that speed will encourage a pony to cover more ground. It won't. Hurrying the pony actually results in *shorter* strides and gives the impression that you're mounted on a rabbit or a pogo stick. Besides being completely antithetical to the process of dressage, this is not likely to impress any judge of an under saddle class; nor will it better your chances of making the lines between fences. At best you'll find yourself adding a stride wherever you go; at worst you'll constantly be arriving at your fences on the half-stride. And in the dressage arena, your lengthening will be nil. *Slow* the pony's pace first. Encourage it to bend, round, carry more weight on its rear end where it belongs by continuing the work outlined above, and *then* ask it to move forward again with *longer*, not *quicker*, strides that are more rhythmic and even. Now when you increase your pace you'll get a powerful forward thrust and a lengthening of the stride rather than a faster footfall. Likewise, when you ask for a shortened stride, it will feel collected and bouncy rather than quick and flat.

MAKING THE DISTANCES: FURTHER HELP IN JUMPING

A rolling hayfield is a wonderful place to work on the next step for the pony competing over fences, which is teaching both of you how to maintain a steady pace up, down, and across gentle slopes without lugging, sucking back, or falling on the forehand. Experiment with moving from canter to hand-gallop and back again while you stay in your half-seat. Again, sweeping circles, serpentines, and figure-eights are very useful. If your pony is still too green or unbalanced to do flying changes of lead, *don't* try to bash or rush it into them. Stay with simple changes until the pony is ready to learn changes properly. Again, most ponies are extremely handy by nature, and many will offer changes themselves when they're balanced and moving freely. Many will even go so far as to change leads automatically according to the slope of the ground, and I have one myself that had to be taught how *not* to change leads at will when in the hack classes to give

Given the proper foundation, some individuals can be competitive at a very high level. Connemara Hideaway's Erin Go Bragh (Hideaway's Erin Smithereen x Hideaway's Centerfold) has an enviable record at the upper levels of combined training with rider Carol Kozlowski. *Photo: CLIX.*

himself a rest. Ponies are catty on their feet. Details like flying changes will come easily to them once balance and rhythm are established.

This work in the field will also give you a solid clue as to what your pony's optimum pace is and how far up it can be adjusted without becoming unbalanced, flat, or rapid. In

219

competition, it's likely that you'll be riding more forward to the fences than riders on 16-hand horses, and work on slopes will help develop the strength and coordination required to maintain the pace the pony needs to maintain to make the longer distances between fences smoothly and efficiently.

Gymnastics are vital for the pony whose stride is somewhat shorter than the ideal. A pony that is hurried to its fences may get into the habit of chipping in consistently, which can be hard to break. Or if it's the sort that doesn't like to get too close to anything, it may simply leave from distances too long to give anything but a flat, weak jump. Gymnastics encourage a correct jumping style as well as developing your pony's and your own eye for achieving comfortable distances. Gymnastics don't have to be high to be effective; in fact, they should always be simple and straightforward. Again, there are numerous valuable books that illustrate the various valuable combinations of gymnastics that will best help you and your pony to progress. But when in doubt, trotting poles followed by an X or a little vertical; or an X to a small vertical eighteen feet away to a small oxer another eighteen feet away are both good exercises. *Don't* try to increase the distance to twenty-four feet or twenty-six feet! Remember that those distances are designed to be met by a horse galloping *forward*, not approaching a simple gymnastic at a trot. Distances that are too long will only encourage a flat, weak jumping style, or at worst back your pony off so that it adds a stride to protect itself. Stick with the basics, and let your pony learn them well. You'll find that it will pay you back handsomely when you come around that awkward corner in the Hunter stake seeing nothing and your pony finds the distance for you.

While riding ponies against horses means riding with less margin for error and more precision than might be necessary on something at least a foot taller, it doesn't mean that the pony can't do it. Stride length is not tied to scope or athleticism, especially at the adult amateur levels, and neither good jumpers nor good dressage prospects are size- or breed-specific. Given the proper desire, enough talent, and a commitment to proper training, most ponies can be helped in their ability to improve on their already considerable natural talents.

Chapter

14

THE IMPORTANCE OF THE PONY AS A FOUNDATION

We owe a lot to ponies. Over the centuries, they have served our ancestors as a means of transport, a source of food and income, and a beast of burden whose labors often replaced that of humans. In some remote parts of the world, they still serve these purposes. And for the rest of us, they have provided ourselves and our children with many hours of pleasure, comfort, and safety in every possible capacity. They have asked for (and frequently received) very little in return.

The very natural and man-made adversities (mentioned in Chapter 2) that have threatened to wipe out their populations on numerous occasions throughout the years has in fact given modern breeders, riders, and drivers a gift of lasting value that we in the United States are still only beginning to appreciate. This gift exists in the historically rich genetic diversity and enduring qualities that are still carried prominently in the heredity of our pony breeds.

In our tendency to breed animals ever bigger and more refined to meet ever more specific uses, we've lost much in the way of intelligence, hardiness of constitution, soundness of limbs and feet, and the willingness to do what's asked cheerfully. When turning our gaze to ponies, the goal has been to try to improve and refine on them in the same way we've done with horses, until they look like nothing more than miniaturized versions of the larger breeds. Our idea of a great compliment is to describe a pony as not being like a pony at all, but more like a little Thoroughbred, Arab, warmblood, or whatever. Having used the horse to improve the pony, and using the pony more or less solely for its size, we call the result a better animal.

Better at what, we might ask? The "improved" pony, frequently seen at the top shows where it excels and for which it is largely bred, is certainly more beautiful and refined than its native cousin, and its daisy cutting movement is certainly more spectacular. But the newer types of ponies have not necessarily been able to pass on any attributes that might be considered beneficial to their further offspring or for many of the people who will ride and handle them. Some have become too hot for the children that they profess to be suited for, except in the confines of an arena under the eye and care of a professional trainer. Others are now heir to the same lameness, conditions, and temperamental uncertainties that mark their larger cousins. Many have lost the innate sense, athletic ability, and agility that have always been hallmarks of the pony as an all-round performer and ultimately safe conveyance in situations ranging from the traditional (hacking, hunting, etc.) to the odd (step stools from which to peer into bird's nests and any other of the myriad uses thought up by creative children).

In constantly selecting breeding stock for its refinement and movement to the exclusion of temperament, soundness, brains, and durability, we have actually endangered the root stock of many native breeds. The classic nonequine example is that of hens and cows bred so specifically for so long to be high producers of eggs and milk respectively that they have lost any sort of mothering instinct. Hens won't sit on eggs. Cows become difficult calvers and indifferent mothers. In the equine realm, it's just as easy to cite the notorious example of the Quarter Horse's feet, or the old standard of Morgan that is now such a rarity. The genes that govern "old-fashioned" traits can be (in some instances have been) bred completely out of animals that no longer bear any resemblance to their foundation stock. The same can be said for many of the ponies that arrived here several generations ago, as witnessed by the American Shetland. *Once these genes are gone, they are gone forever. They cannot be replaced.* They have become extinct.

How Breed Type Is Lost

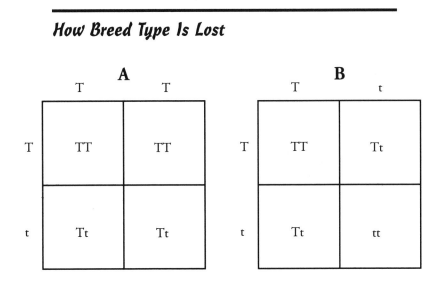

In example A, two typical individuals of a breed are mated, but one of them is true breed type (TT), while the other carries one allele for more refinement (t). While all of the resulting offspring will appear typical of their breed standard, 50 percent will carry alleles (and possibly show some sign of) added refinement. If the Tt offspring are subsequently bred to typical or "old fashioned" members of the breed, the result will still be 50 percent. If they are bred to other more refined ponies, the result will be different, as shown in example B: 25 percent typical, 50 percent typical with more refinement, and 25 percent no longer true to type. Breed the nontypical (tt) offspring to a Tt pony (C), and the following can be expected:

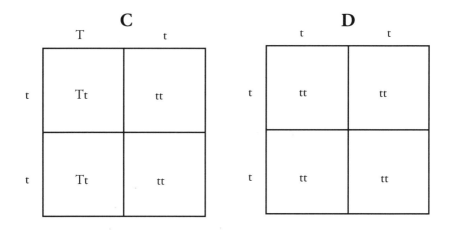

50 percent still typical but more refined, and 50 percent not true to traditional type. Breed the nontypical member to another nontypical pony (D), and in four generations you have eliminated all the benefits of centuries of natural selection. Once it is gone, the genes to return do not exist. They are, in essence, extinct. Preservation of original type is thus essential to the genetic health of a breed.

Nature, that harshest of all genetic selectors, has created in native pony breeds animals that have proven themselves through many generations to be innately hardy, healthy, intelligent, adaptable both physically and mentally, sound, and generally free from the numerous flaws, weaknesses, and tendencies to illness that stalk many of the larger breeds. It's more common than not to see one of these ponies staying sound enough to teach literally two or three generations of children and adults the fine points of riding. While it's treated as a cause for celebration (and the basis of a great ad campaign) if a Thoroughbred or other sport horse retires to stud sound, hundreds of proud pony owners talk of stallions and mares that have carried them in the hunt field, eventing, or in competitive trail well into their twenties, sound and with legs remarkably unblemished, while simultaneously siring or producing foals. And it's not an infrequent occurrence to see a well-loved old pony still patiently teaching beginners how to post in its thirtieth year. Ponies, in short, are *expected* to retire sound, if they retire at all. For this and many other reasons, many proponents of fullbred ponies never consider crossbreeding as an option within their favored breeds because, as one prominent breeder maintains, "We feel we already have a totally versatile pony that fulfills all of our requirements. Frankly, he couldn't get any better."

Regaining Breed Type

<table>
<tr><td colspan="3" align="center">A</td></tr>
<tr><td></td><td align="center">t</td><td align="center">t</td></tr>
<tr><td>T</td><td>Tt</td><td>Tt</td></tr>
<tr><td>t</td><td>tt</td><td>tt</td></tr>
</table>

<table>
<tr><td colspan="3" align="center">B</td></tr>
<tr><td></td><td align="center">T</td><td align="center">t</td></tr>
<tr><td>T</td><td>TT</td><td>Tt</td></tr>
<tr><td>t</td><td>Tt</td><td>tt</td></tr>
</table>

As examples A and B show, regaining breed type can be a time consuming and difficult process if there are no longer any TT (or, as they are sometimes referred to, "old-fashioned" types) which are preponent for passing on the diminished attributes of the breed in question. The second generation will have a somewhat "scrambled egg" appearance—25 percent typical, 50 percent typical but showing some form of refinement, and 25 percent nontypical ponies. The 50 percent that are Tt will always carry a 25 percent probability of producing more tt (nontypical ponies) if bred to other Tts. Using the 25 percent that are TT on further generations, however, will yield a different result, as seen in examples C and D.

C

	t	t
T	Tt	Tt
T	Tt	Tt

D

	T	t
T	TT	Tt
T	TT	Tt

In example C, 100 percent typical but more refined. In example D, 50 percent true breed type again, capable of predictably passing on the best characteristics of that breed.

The figures above are also an excellent illustration of how outside blood is eventually assimilated into a breed—a period of one or several generations (depending on further care being taken in selection of breeding stock) in which type may be seen as erratic, followed by a period of greater uniformity that includes the characteristics desired from the outcross. This is how most warmbloods have been created.

But it's equally important to recognize the limitations of the native. In the larger context of upper-level competition, it's very rare to find them competing to the highest echelon. Their size, and sometimes their build, is against them, as we've mentioned before. Yet here the pony's strength can still be felt, as an essential ingredient in the development of sound and beautiful crossbred ponies and sport horses whose heritages represent the best of both worlds, and that are bred precisely to achieve those great competitive heights.

The point is not so much that one style of animal must be better than another. Nor is it that all should be either bred up or bred down to look like another according to the current fashion or whim. The point is rather that the improved ponies and refined horses demand and can benefit from the enduring qualities of the original native pony to maintain or reintroduce all of that which is good about the traditional types. These characteristics are necessary to the genetic health and continued prosperity of all ponies and horses. In the British Isles, many breeders of very fancy crossbred show ponies admit freely that they must dip back into the native pony rootstock periodically to regain the qualities that have made these ponies the ideal mount for children through the generations, and that in fact there is such a thing as too much improvement. As time goes on, these breeders have grown to see their Mountain and Moorland ponies more and more as national treasures, and with good reason: Scratch the pedigrees of many really successful international British show jumpers or eventers and you'll find a Connemara, Welsh, Exmoor, or other native pony in its background somewhere. The value of using pony crosses to create horses with the scope and attitude to compete at the upper levels of any equine discipline while retaining sound long enough to stay there for a period of years has been well documented in those countries. A British hall of fame listing "pony-improved horses" would contain such historic names as The Nugget, High and Mighty, Foxhunter, Stroller, Dundrum, Eagle Rock, and Little Model. Most recently, none other than the immortal Milton (reputed to have been sired by a well-known Connemara teaser) and the halfbred Welsh Cobs Everest Jet Lag and Charlie Brummell stand out in the ranks of British jumping stars. In the United States we've had horses like Marcus Aurelius (long known as "The Bionic Pony"), The Grasshopper, St. Finbarr, and Tre Awain Belfast in the ranks of half-pony eventers that have made it to the very top of that demanding sport. The performances of Seldom Seen and Last Scene have inspired a host of aspiring dressage riders whose

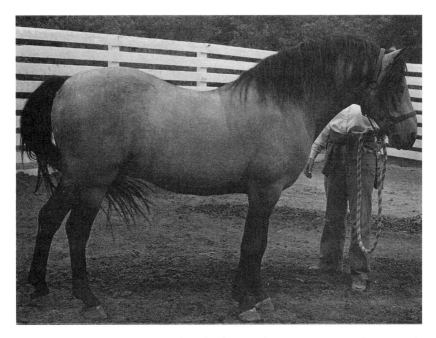

The Connemara Tre Awain Roderick O'Conor (MacDara x *Lonely Cottage), pictured at age twenty-five, illustrates the "old-fashioned" characteristics of bone, ruggedness, and temperament required to produce sound, sane, and enduring athletes.

mounts are not giant warmbloods. And pony-cross teams have been well represented both in the United States and abroad in international pairs driving competition. This list is by no means exhaustive. But it's sad that some of the people who compete with these marvelous crossbreds are slow to acknowledge the part that isn't Thoroughbred, Arab, or warmblood, feeling that it should be hidden. Each one of these wonderful animals owes a great debt to the pony that makes up half of its heritage. This deserves to be a matter of pride.

It's true that a pony like the very ancient Exmoor leaves a great deal to be desired in our modern idealization of ponies and horses whose make-up replicates that of the Thoroughbred in its grace, stride, fire, and speed; or the warmblood with its

His half Thoroughbred son Tre Awain Belfast was long listed for the 1984 U.S. Three Day Team with owner-rider Nancy Winter. *Photo: Winter.*

inspiring movement; or the Arab in its legendary beauty and strength over long distances. With our relatively uneducated and unappreciative eyes, we might even find the little Exmoor a sad comparison—too common in the head, too strongly intelligent (and as a result, opinionated), too short in the neck, straight in the shoulder, long in the back, and too round in its movement.

Yet the same Exmoor is so hardy that it can usually live outside in the worst weather imaginable and subsist very nicely without grain, stabling, and heavy blankets. It can carry more weight for its size than anything short of a draft horse ever could. It can handle trappy, rocky, and boggy country cleverly and at speed without falling or going lame. It's smart enough to know how to protect itself, to pick its own line, and to get out of trouble in tricky situations. It has the competitive spark that makes it anything but dull as a ride for skilled pony clubbers and small adults with the ambition to "run and jump." And it has the immense tolerance of all native ponies that allows it to put up with and forgive the inevitable mistakes of children and novice riders.

Field hunters, eventers, endurance riders, packers, heads of handicapped riding programs, and reinsmen alike covet these attributes in their constant search for the ideal sport horse. The fact that they are all present to a great degree in nearly all native pony breeds thus argues strongly for their use as a foundation in the breeding of superior sport horses. In the British Isles, it's considered to be a great addition to have upwards of 25 percent native blood in a sport horse (or sometimes more, if the size is adequate). This is thought to be enough to optimize the native characteristics while retaining the size, scope, and speed of the hot-blooded horse being used in the cross.

It even leads to the contemplation that in fact, we've been looking at the equation through the wrong end of the telescope. Instead of seeing the horse as an improvement on the pony, perhaps we ought to be thinking of the pony as an improvement on the horse.

APPRECIATING THE NATIVES

With the best will in the world, it's true that many of the strengths of traditional native ponies are lost in translation when the ponies are removed both from native soils and from the strict standards of societies whose members are accustomed to seeing certain conformation types as a matter of course. What American breeder who loves ponies without having been acclimated to the old-fashioned look of a true-to-standard Connemara wouldn't be confused, if all his or her previous experience had been with the crossbred ponies showing on the AHSA-A hunter pony circuit? What American judge could be expected to understand native breed type if hunter or warmblood breeding classes were all he or she has experienced before? An important facet of preserving the qualities of these

The ability of crossbred ponies such as Woodlands Welcome (King's Cavalier x Woodlands Queen of Queens) to succeed at the highest levels of pony hunter competition is well documented. *Photo: Ed Keller.*

When the larger pony breeds are crossed with Thoroughbreds and warm-bloods, equally talented and successful show hunters can result, as Connie Tuor has found with her half Connemara Precious Stone. *Photo: Jim Bortvedt.*

ponies is first learning how to look at them, then to understand the meaning and importance of their chief characteristics in the light of a whole breed heritage before meddling further in any attempts to improve on their outward appearance. Maintaining and learning to appreciate the distinct type that identifies any mountain and moorland pony thus involves understanding the influence that environment and necessity have had on our chosen breed's development.

What we see as old-fashioned characteristics (sometimes a euphemism for "common") need not refer to a lack of quality. *Quality and refinement are not necessarily the same thing.* We have only to look at some of the European warmbloods to see walking examples of quality going hand in hand with large frames, big bone, and a certain massiveness of build. We need to turn the same eye to our ponies, and give them the same credit for both ruggedness and beauty.

Then we need to educate judges, who all too often are accustomed only to the conformation hunter as a model of physical correctness and appeal, and who frequently become responsible for determining what kind of animals we breed, both by the way they pin in-hand classes and by the way we respond by trying to change our standards to fit this often rather subjective and arbitrary method of assessment. If we are to make any headway at all in preserving breed type in its many forms, we must hone our ability to see the subtleties of type that make each breed a distinct entity, and encourage judges to do the same. It isn't enough that *we* know what we're breeding for. We must also teach judges how to see what we're seeing, and to recognize its importance. Then, when we are called upon to judge in our own right, we need to be absolutely certain of our priorities in choosing the best animals on the day. If type is what we're looking for, type must be what takes precedence—even over that absolutely gorgeous thing at the end of the line that placed at Devon last year. It's hard, but if she doesn't look like she belongs to the rest of "the family," she has to go down the line a bit, and let the truer-to-type individuals take the top. This, too, is how we protect and promote the distinct and valuable qualities that mark each of our pony breeds.

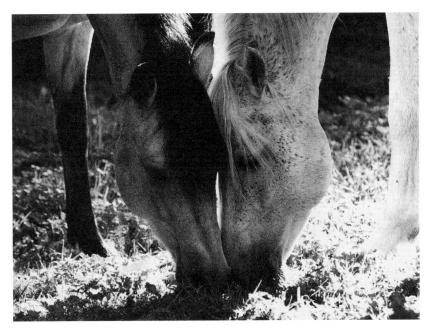

In assigning credit to these superb athletes, the influence of the native pony in the back field like Connemaras Ros Na Ri Moira and Tre Awain Ginger Blue should never be underestimated. *Photo: Kathryn Roe.*

THE FUTURE OF THE PONY

In many ways, the future of ponies has never looked brighter in the United States. Their role as the ideal first mounts of children ranging from short stirrup to the upper levels of pony club remains assured. Their increased popularity as viable alternatives for adult amateurs can be seen as nothing but positive. Perhaps it's safe to say that we're beginning to realize that the pony in all its varied forms is very much worth being treasured on its own merits.

This is good news for breeders who love ponies and want to produce more of them for a waiting world. And it's good news for our ponies, which have survived eons on their own considerable genetic strengths. They deserve no less than our best efforts to ensure that these are allowed to continue and thrive.

Appendix

SOURCES OF
FURTHER INFORMATION

No matter how long we stay in the pony business, there is always more to learn and there are still pieces of information that we need access to quickly nearly everyday. In the interest of developing a good, basic reference library, here are some books that have stood the test of time and proven useful to thousands of breeders of all types. Obviously, there are numerous other titles that may do as well, but these are the ones I'm most familiar with.

BOOKS

Blanchard, Tony L. and Dickson D. Varner, eds. *Stallion Management.* Philadelphia: W. E. B. Saunders, 1992.
> When you need absolutely up-to-date technical information about breeding, this volume from the *Veterinary Clinics of North America: Equine Practice* series is a terrific source. It's actually much easier to read than you might think, even though it's essentially a reference work for practicing vets who do a lot of reproductive work. There isn't much it doesn't cover, and the sections on semen

collection and artificial insemination techniques are especially valuable to anybody who intends to do a lot of this.

British Horse Society and Pony Club. *Choosing and Buying the Pony.* London: British Horse Society and Pony Club, 1990.

―――. *Keeping a Pony at Grass,* 4th ed. London: British Horse Society and Pony Club, 1985.

―――. *The Manual of Horsemanship,* 10th ed. London: British Horse Society and Pony Club, 1993.

―――. *Training Young Horses.* London: British Horse Society and Pony Club, 1990.

> This series, which has been regularly revised, updated, and enlarged over many years, is still one of the best sources of good, basic, *practical* information on pony-keeping to be found anywhere. Although obviously written from the British standpoint, a great deal of the information is easily transferrable to a North American application. Common sense and practicality are stressed, which in this technocratic age is very refreshing. And the British are unquestionably much more accustomed to understanding and tailoring information to the specific needs of ponies, which makes these volumes doubly valuable to any pony breeder.

Dent, Anthony, and Daphne Machin Goodall. *A History of the British Native Ponies.* London: J. A. Allen, 1988.

> This absolutely wonderful history of native breeds and their evolution covers an immense timespan from the Bronze Age to the early part of the twentieth century. Even if you aren't a history buff it may turn you into one, and the story of how native ponies developed and maintained their qualities is fascinating. The book is also an eloquent plea to treasure the ponies' native characteristics and the gene pools that have managed to survive throughout the ages with so many of their attributes all but unchanged. A great argument for preservation.

Hardman, A. C. Leighton. *Stallion Management: A Practical Guide for Stud Owners.* London: Pelham Books, 1974; Hollywood: Wilshire Book Co., 1974.

> This book is out of print and may be difficult to locate, which is too bad, because it's a good one. Just as the title suggests, its emphasis is on the practical aspects of dealing with stallions (and also mares). While written from the British perspective, there is

much to interest U.S. breeders, and the sections on promotion, records, management of outside mares, and handling a novice breeding stallion are particularly valuable to the small breeder.

Harris, Susan E. *Grooming to Win*. 2d ed. New York: Howell Book House, 1991.

This excellent book first came out in 1977 and has pretty much proven itself to be a standard for getting a horse or pony into show condition. Since appearance has a lot to with whether or not we're successful in marketing our stock, an understanding of how to turn ponies out properly for their public appearances is essential.

————. *The U.S. Pony Club Manuals*. New York: Howell Book House, 1994.

The first of these terrific manuals, for the "D" level, came out in 1994. The manual for the "C" level is new in 1995. Styled after the invaluable series put out by the British Horse Society, they were written specifically to reflect American attitudes and methods, which is very useful. The manuals have already been accepted for use by both the U.S. and Canadian Pony Clubs, and subsequent volumes will be dedicated to the "B" and "A" levels.

Hayes, Horace M. *Veterinary Notes for Horse Owners*. 17th ed. Revised and updated by Peter Rossdale. New York: Prentice Hall Press, 1987.

A great old standard that includes everything you ever wanted to know (and some things that you wish you didn't) in the realm of veterinary information, kept up to date throughout a printing career that has spanned a century.

Hayes, Karen E. N. *The Complete Book Of Foaling: An Illustrated Guide for the Foaling Attendant*. New York: Howell Book House, 1993.

This is a newcomer to the world of breeding books, and a good one to keep around. It does cover territory that has been dealt with elsewhere, such as prenatal care of the mare, the various stages of labor, delivery, and so forth. But the labor and delivery parts are really well done, with lots of good illustrations, and the information that deals with the foal's critical first twelve hours is must reading for all pony breeders.

Kellon, Eleanor M. *First Aid for Horses*. Millwood, N.Y.: Breakthrough, 1989.

Another really good volume, but more basic and easier to use than the above. It has the great advantage of being color-coded, so that you can look things up *quickly* when you need to. This is the kind of book you keep in the tack room for immediate access after you're done reading it the first time.

Lose, M. Phyllis. *Blessed Are the Brood Mares.* 2d ed. New York: Howell Book House, 1991.

First published in 1971, this book has become a classic. It has everything a breeder needs to know about caring for the mare from breeding through foaling, including both the practical and the medical aspects of keeping broodmares happy, healthy, and productive. All of this information has been revised in the latest edition, so that it's pretty well up to the minute as far as the veterinary aspects go, and a new chapter on difficult foaling situations has been added.

Rooney, James R. *The Mechanics of the Horse.* Melbourne, Fla.: Krieger, 1981.

This is a useful source of easily digestible technical information dealing with the mechanics of how structure relates to soundness, movement, athletic ability, etc. Whether you're of a scientific bent or just want to know *why* Old Flossie moves the way she does, this is a great primer on the topic.

Rossdale, Peter. *Horse Breeding.* North Pomfret, Vt.: Trafalgar Square, 1992.

Another breeding book that's been around for some time (it first appeared in 1981) and has proven valuable to a great number of people. It's a wonderful book, full of information that manages to present the technical and genetic side of breeding without losing sight of the down to earth.

Russell, Valerie. *Judging Horses and Ponies.* London: Pelham Books, 1978.

If you can find this book, grab it. Its descriptions of the conformation, way of going, strengths, and weaknesses of British native pony breeds are really valuable, as are its comments on the judging of these breeds (the book also encompasses hunters, hacks, Arabs, and draft breeds). Its approach is totally matter of fact and very down to earth. Easy to learn from and interesting to read.

Wagoner, Don, ed. *Breeding Management and Foal Development.* Grand Prairie, Tex.: Equine Research Publications, 1982.

Another volume in the very useful series from Equine Research, it also contains an immense amount of highly informative and technical yet accessible information that is essential to any breeder.

Wagoner, Don M. *Equine Genetics and Selection Procedures.* Grand Prairie, Tex.: Equine Research Publications, 1978.
> For a basic in-depth and comprehensible introduction to equine genetics, this volume is hard to beat. It explains in detail the ins and outs of selection, heritability, inbreeding, outcrossing, and so on. For those with an interest in color breeding, its section on color inheritance is fascinating. It's extremely easy to read and the information in it is quickly accessible. It also has a useful glossary that gives clear definitions of all the technical terms used throughout the book, which will keep you from going cross-eyed with confusion.

ORGANIZATIONS

This list of organizations is not complete, but it will give you a start on where to go for the kinds of information you're bound to need. In addition to the national organizations mentioned, it's strongly recommended that you support your state or regional groups. Only by grassroots support can we all survive and thrive.

American Driving Society, P.O. Box 160, Metamora, MI 48455; (810) 233-8666
> Governing body for driven equestrian sports in the United States.

American Horse Council, 1700 K St. N.W., Washington, D.C. 20006; (202) 296-4031
> The equine industry's voice in Washington. Among its many good works is the annual *Horse Industry Directory*, which has more information on organizations and publications than any other listing source available. It also oversees the American Youth Horse Council.

American Horse Shows Association, 220 East 42nd St., New York, NY 10017-5876; (212) 972-2472
> Governing body and umbrella organization for equestrian sports in the United States. Oversees Horse of the Year Awards and year-end Zone Awards as well as FEI competition in the United States. Among the pony breeds recognized by the AHSA are Welsh, Shetland, Hackney, and Connemara.

American Livestock Breeds Conservancy, Box 477, Pittsboro, NC 27312; (919) 542-5704

Oversees registries for Exmoors, Gotlands, and Dales ponies in the United States; a voice for genetic diversity and the preservation of threatened breeds of domestic livestock of all kinds.

National 4-H Council, 7100 Connecticut Ave., Chevy Chase, MD 20815; (301) 961-2800
Broad-based organization offering horsemastership education for children and teens as well as local, regional, and national competitions in judging, showmanship, and equitation in all seats.

U.S. Combined Training Association, Inc., P.O. Box 2247, Leesburg, VA 22075; (703) 779-0440
Governing body for eventing in the United States. Has initiated an all-breeds award system in which several pony breeds are taking part.

U.S. Dressage Federation, P.O. Box 80668, Lincoln, NE 68501; (402) 434-8550
Governing body for dressage in the United States. It initiated the first all-breeds awards program, which has been very successful. Many pony breeds are represented.

U.S. Pony Clubs, Inc., 4071 Iron Works Pike, Lexington, KY 40511; (606) 254-7669
National organization offering juniors horsemastership skills through all levels of expertise in combined training, jumping, and dressage. Offers test for ratings at levels "D" through "A" as well as regional and national team and individual competitions in combined training, jumping, dressage, tetrathlon, and games.

BREED SOCIETIES

Alberta Pony and Small Horse Promotional Group, Box 4, Site 2, RR 1, Strathmore, Alberta T0J 3H0 Canada; (403) 934-3666

American Connemara Pony Society, Contact: Marynell Eyles, 2630 Hunting Ridge Rd., Winchester, VA 22603; (703) 662-5953
For information in Canada, contact Doris Jacobi, Box 53A, RR 1, So. Edmonton, Alberta T6H 4N6; (403) 955-2097

American Exmoor Pony Registry, American Livestock Breeds Conservancy, P.O. Box 477, Pittsboro, NC 27312-0477; (919) 542-5704

American Shetland Pony Club and American Miniature Horse Registry, Contact: Barbara A. Stockwell, P.O. Box 3415, Peoria, IL 61614-3415; (309) 691-9661

American Welara Pony Society, Contact: Gail and John Collins, P.O. Box 401, Yucca Valley, CA 92286; (619) 364-2048

Canadian Mountain and Moorland Society (Dales and Exmoor Ponies), Contact: Anne Holmes, RR #4, Box 273, Amherst, Nova Scotia B4H 3Y2, Canada; (902) 661-7250

Dartmoor Pony Society of America, Contact: Linda Lucas, 1005 Pearl Wood Rd., Albany, OH 45710; (614) 698-6497

Haflinger Association of America, Contact: Beatrice Wallace, 14570 Gratiot Rd., Hemlock, MI 48626-9416; (517) 642-5307

Haflinger Registry of North America, Contact: Jewel Woodward, 14640 State Route 83, Coshocton, OH 43812; (614) 829-2790

Maritime Small Horse and Pony Association, Contact: Afiena Kamminga, 453 Maplewood, RR 1, Millville, New Brunswick, NS EOH 1MO; (506) 463-8164

National Chincoteague Pony Association, 2595 Jensen Rd., Bellingham, WA 98226; (206) 671-8338

National Quarter Pony Association, Contact: Richard Ekin, P.O. Box 922, Galion, OH 44833; (419) 468-6591

New Forest Pony Association, Inc., Contact: Jody Waltz, P.O. Box 638, Harrisville, RI 02830-0638

Norwegian Fjord Horse Registry, Contact: Joel Hempel, Skoal Farm, P.O. Box 38, Gilmanton Iron Works, NH 03837; (603) 364-7757

Pony of the Americas Club, Contact: Clyde Goff, 5240 Elmwood Ave., Indianapolis, IN 46203-5990; (317) 788-0107

Swedish Gotland Breeders Society, Contact: Leslie Bebensee, Route 3, Box 134, Corinth, KY 41010; (606) 234-5707

Welsh Pony and Cob Society of America, Contact: Lisa A. Landis, P.O. Box 2977, Winchester, VA 22604; (703) 667-6195

Welsh Pony and Cob Society of Canada, Contact: Beverly Morton-Olafson, Box 254 Beeton, Ontario L0G 1A0, Canada

INDEX

A

Abortion, 123, 146, 147
Advertising, 200–205, 208
A.G.I.D. *See* Coggins test
Alleles, 63, 71–74
Andalusian, 12, 17, 19
Anthelmintics, classes of, 152
Antibodies, 144, 177
Arabian, 12, 15, 19, 20, 22, 33, 41, 42, 44, 228
Ascarids, 151

B

Barb, 12, 15, 19, 33, 44
Barns, 137–38
Blankets and sheets, 134–36
Bots, 151–52
Breeding, 3–5, 8
  artificial insemination, 166–68
  contracts, 171–75
  hand breeding, 161–66
  pasture breeding, 158–61
  preparation of mares for, 162–65, 167–71, 173

preparation of stallions for, 162–65
scheduling of, 164–66, 169
Breeding roll, 161
Breed societies, 16. *See also* individual breeds
Breed standards
  adherence, to 5–6, 44–45
  Connemara, 21–22
  development of, 11–12
  Exmoor, 228–30
  Haflinger, 25
  in mares, 86–88
  Norwegian Fjord, 28–29
  related to environment, 14
  Shetland, 32
  in stallions, 111–12
  Welsh Sections A and B, 37–38
  Welsh Sections C and D, 38–39
  See also Native type
Brochures, 206–8
Broodmares
  assessment of pedigrees, 62
  care after foaling, 179
  estrus (heat) cycle, 159
  feeding, 126, 128
  gestation, 176